MARATHON TRAINING

MARATHON TRAINING

The Proven 100-Day Program for Success

Joe Henderson

West Coast Editor, *Runner's World*
Editor, *Running Commentary*

Human Kinetics

Library of Congress Cataloging-in-Publication Data

Henderson, Joe, 1943-
    Marathon training : the proven 100-day program for success / Joe
Henderson.
        p.   cm.
    ISBN 0-88011-591-2
    1. Marathon running--Training.   I. Title.
    GV1065.17.T73H45   1997
    796.42'5--DC20   96-43355
                                                                   CIP

ISBN: 0-88011-591-2

Developmental Editor: Kristine Enderle; **Assistant Editors:** Coree Schutter and Sandra Merz Bott; **Copyeditor:**   Bob Replinger; **Proofreader:** Jim Burns; **Graphic Designer:** Robert Reuther; **Graphic Artist:** Julie Overholt; **Photo Editor:** Boyd LaFoon; **Cover Designer:** Jack Davis; **Cover Photographer:** © Photo Run; **Printer:** United Graphics

Human Kinetics books are available at special discounts for bulk purchase. Special editions or book excerpts can also be created to specification. For details, contact the Special Sales Manager at Human Kinetics.

Printed in the United States of America   10   9   8   7   6   5

Human Kinetics
Web site: www.humankinetics.com

United States: Human Kinetics, P.O. Box 5076, Champaign, IL 61825-5076
800-747-4457
e-mail: humank@hkusa.com

Canada: Human Kinetics, 475 Devonshire Road, Unit 100, Windsor, ON N8Y 2L5
800-465-7301 (in Canada only)
e-mail: orders@hkcanada.com

Europe: Human Kinetics, Units C2/C3 Wira Business Park, West Park Ring Road
Leeds LS16 6EB, United Kingdom
+44 (0) 113 278 1708
e-mail: hk@hkeurope.com

Australia: Human Kinetics, 57A Price Avenue, Lower Mitcham, South Australia 5062
08 8277 1555
e-mail: liahka@senet.com.au

New Zealand: Human Kinetics, P.O. Box 105-231, Auckland Central
09-523-3462
e-mail: hkp@ihug.co.nz

To Fred Lebow, for opening New York City's streets
to marathoners and for leading hundreds of thousands
of them on this journey.

CONTENTS

Today marathons welcome all runners—old and young, male and female, fairly fast and very slow. For most, surviving the distance is just as noble as finishing fast and setting records.

INTRODUCTION:
Your Marathon

I am a marathoner—never a fast one and never a contender for any prize, but none of that really matters. The marathon is less a race for records and prizes than it is a survival test that rewards all who finish. I've survived dozens of these events.

Like everyone who has ever run a marathon, I have a story to tell. Before starting to advise you on how to write a much more important story—your own—permit me to relate my small tale. It reflects my feelings about this marvelous event as a whole.

I love marathoning as a sport, and love no single marathon more than Boston. That's partly because it is the ancestral home of marathoning in the United States, but especially because it was my birthplace as a marathoner. Boston 1967 was my first try at this distance.

A first marathon is like a first love. You might bumble through it, but you never forget it. Nothing you do later will ever be quite as memorable as your initiation, even if its memories are painful.

Mine aren't. My first marathon wasn't the fiasco that I'd heard was the birthright of first timers. It was perfect. Perfect in training (an accidentally ideal mix of long runs, fast runs, and rest) and execution. (What Heartbreak Hill? What 20-mile Wall?) It was too perfect to show what marathoning really is.

Maybe I should have stopped with the first one. It would have given me a perfect career: a surprisingly good time and an amazingly trouble-free run in the most historic of marathons. But that isn't how love works. You taste it once and want more. You go for more, and reality sets in.

Boston's course and conditions are record makers and record spoilers. The weather either helps or hurts. I ran my coldest and hottest marathon there, which were also my fastest and slowest. The early downhill miles at Boston either produce a fast finish or wreck it with a too-fast start. One year I combined my best first half and worst second half.

I never would better that first Boston time. No marathon would ever go as smoothly as that one did. But I've come back to the marathon more than 40 times. You don't dump an old love after inevitably seeing the imperfections.

Multiply my memories by the tens of thousands of people who have ever run at Boston, and the hundreds of thousands who've run other marathons, and you begin to understand our collective love affair with this event. The marathon celebrates a double centennial as the 20th century nears its finish.

© Photo Run / Victor Sailer

A view of the marathon that few runners ever get to see: the empty road ahead for leaders at the Boston Marathon.

The marathon as a race (as opposed to a tale from Greek mythology) was born at the first modern Olympics in Athens, 1896. The oldest annual marathon, Boston, marked its 100th running in 1996.

Throughout its first century, the marathon has stood as a centerpiece of the Olympics. It has served as a yearly rite of spring in Boston all that time. But until recently, the race attracted little attention anywhere else.

Then came the running boom of the 1970s and 1980s, first in the United States and then around the world. The marathon grew up, exploding in both number and size. New runners created the need for more races. New races spawned still more runners. Every city of size conducted a marathon of its own—with London, New York City, Honolulu, and Los Angeles attracting fields of twenty thousand or more.

Marathons changed in character as well as size. Up front the leaders ran for prize money. Farther back in the field came runners old and young, male and female, fairly fast and very slow. The event welcomed them all. For most, this wasn't a race but a survival test. Surviving became a form of winning—just as noble in its own way as finishing first and setting records.

This attitude helps explain the still-growing appeal of the marathon. At the start of its second century, more than three hundred thousand runners now go this distance each year in the United States alone. This is triple the number of marathoners in 1980, when running's popularity was thought to have peaked.

The marathon, which is about enduring and surviving, has endured and survived. By running one, you become part of a long and proud history. You join a parade of marathoners that reaches from the 19th century almost to the 21st.

But enough rhapsodizing. Let's get down to the realities of running a marathon.

The thought of covering 26.2 miles on foot is as frightening as it is fascinating. The act itself might appear as simple as putting one foot in front of the other and remembering to alternate feet. But doing this for hours on end can seriously test your mental as well as physical resources.

A marathon takes anywhere from a little over two hours to a lot more than four hours to complete. The event drains your fluid and fuel reserves. It hammers your feet and legs. It makes you wonder at some point late in the race, "What am I doing here?"

Marathoning involves the whole family. This young fan awaits her favorite runner at the Chicago Marathon.

What happens during the marathon is neither the beginning nor the end of your work. You've invested several months of training into getting here, and you'll spend another month or more getting over this effort.

So you see that the decision to run a marathon is not made lightly. It's a major commitment of time and energy. This work can be quite gratifying if done right, or equally distressing if done wrong.

In this book, we try to maximize gratification and minimize distress. But I won't mislead you: there is no easy, risk-free way to run a marathon. If there were, everyone would do it and you wouldn't feel so special. While it's true that hundreds of thousands of people are marathoners, they still represent only about one in a hundred people who enter races, one in a thousand who run at all, and one in ten thousand from the general population.

You don't choose to run a marathon *despite* its difficulty but *because* it is hard. You like the feeling of aiming for a distant goal and eventually reaching it.

You can't fake a marathon. Maybe you can wake up one fine spring morning and decide to run a 5K or 10K that day, trusting your normal few miles of running to carry you through. Try this in a marathon, and the distance will quickly reveal your inadequacies. This event requires special training—and lots of it for a long time.

A victory salute isn't reserved for the first and fastest. Marathoners like this one in Los Angeles can all shout, "I did it!"

Here we focus on those training requirements. This isn't primarily a book about the history or personalities or statistics of the marathon, or about training for any other distance but the marathon. This certainly isn't a primer on running in general, since you must have learned the basics elsewhere before picking up this book. It deals almost exclusively with how to get to and through a race that justifies all the time and effort you put into it.

I've been following marathon-training programs for almost 30 years, and writing them for other runners for nearly 20 years. My first published schedule appeared in a 1977 issue of *Runner's World*. That short article, written in haste, drew more response than all my previous stories combined. Hundreds of marathoners told me of their experiences, positive and otherwise.

I've talked with thousands more runners since then at marathon-training clinics and at races throughout the United States and Canada. They too have let me know what worked—or didn't.

The programs in this book are only distant cousins of those I might have circulated 10, 20, or 30 years ago. The change results partly from runner feedback and partly from influential experimenters such as Tom Osler (who introduced walking breaks to marathoning) and Jeff Galloway (who inspired a whole new way of looking at marathoning).

But marathon programs have changed mostly because of the changes in marathoners in recent decades. Never in the long history of this event has the gap between the fastest and slowest finishers been wider. The median time—equal numbers faster and slower—is now nearly double the winner's time. The late arrivals take three times as long to complete the course as the leaders do.

People enter marathons for many different reasons: to finish any way they can—running, walking, or some mix thereof . . . to run every step . . . to cover the distance faster than they've done it before . . . to qualify for Boston . . . to win an age-group prize or an overall award. (Runners who want to reach the Olympic Trials or win some cash probably operate outside the scope of this book. These elites could write a book of their own.)

For purposes of this book, we split marathoners into three groups. The group you join, and the training program you choose, depends on your experience and goals. We call these groups Cruisers, Pacers, and Racers.

- *Cruisers* aim primarily to finish, and final time doesn't concern them. They enhance their chances of finishing by inserting walking breaks—a technique that noted running author Galloway calls "cruisin'." I recommend that most first timers, and all low-key marathoners, follow the Cruiser training program.

- *Pacers* aim for time goals, or in runners' terms try to set PRs—personal records. They typically run the entire distance, without walking breaks, to maintain their chosen pace. I recommend that runners select the Pacer training program only after cruising their first marathon. (An exception: Runners without marathon experience but an extensive background in short-distance racing can jump directly into Pacer training.)

- *Racers* aim to compete with other marathoners. They race for prizes in their age division or overall. They earn these honors with the hardest training this book has to offer. I recommend the Racer program only to runners whose run-for-time in a previous marathon placed them within sight of the people they want to beat.

© Ken Lee

Marathons come in all sizes and places. These runners sample the rural tranquility of the Napa Valley Marathon.

The lines between these groupings are more blurry than they sound here. You might be a "Cruising Pacer" or a "Pacing Racer" who adjusts your training to fit this blending of goals. Or you might be a Cruiser in your first race, then graduate to Pacing and even to Racing in later marathons. The training plans are flexible enough to accommodate the whole range of ambitions.

Before you start training for your first or fastest or simply next marathon, plot exactly where you're going and how you'll get there. Begin by choosing a race and a training program.

You face a world of choices in marathons. Nearly every country has one, and most U.S. states and Canadian provinces have several. You can find a marathon somewhere any weekend of the year. (See a list of 100 in the back of this book.)

Your choice will depend on factors such as the ease and expense of travel, the time of year, the expected weather and the difficulty of the course, as well as the history of the race and the perks it offers.

Whatever marathon you choose, enter it early. This will seal your commitment to train for it. By knowing exactly where you're going, you also can prepare better. You can study the course map, and run parts of it if you live nearby or mimic its terrain if you don't.

Once you know the race date, count backward by 13 weeks— or 91 days, to be exact. This is where your training begins. (The programs here actually last 100 days. But these include the vital early recovery period after the marathon.)

Now select the training plan that best suits you: Cruiser, Pacer, or Racer. Note that each program has beginning requirements to meet. If you haven't met these standards, do the catch-up work *before* starting this book's training.

Cruisers should have taken a recent nonstop run of one hour or more and run a race of at least 10 kilometers. Pacers should be able to run two hours nonstop, race at least the half-marathon distance and, in most cases, have "cruised" a previous marathon. Racers should have completed a nonstop marathon and be completing long runs of at least two hours when their program begins.

All three programs contain similar ingredients. Only the quantities (and, of course, the speeds) vary.

- *Big day:* one a week for most runners. The long run is most important because it most closely resembles the marathon

© Photo Run / Mike McGevna

Runners cross onto Manhattan Island, midway in the New York City Marathon.

itself, but it isn't the only option. Other choices are a "semi long" run at half the distance of the long one, a fast run of short distance (up to three miles), or a race of up to 10 kilometers.

- *Other training days:* the several easy ones between big days. Here you run by time periods for unknown distance, which helps remove the temptation to race through these workouts. They last 30 to 60 minutes.

- *Rest days:* at least one and as many as three scheduled each week. Cross-training is allowed—in fact, encouraged—on these days. But the effort of swimming, biking, or walking should be less taxing than an easy run.

The ingredients are simple, and the seven recommended sessions each week are flexible. You make the final decision on which days to schedule them and exactly what to run from a range of distances. This gives you wiggle room to set your own pace, to time your runs or go untimed (or to wear a heart monitor), to run on or off roads, to run hills or flats, to run with companions or alone, to rest or run easily or cross-train. It also lets you fit the running into your family and job routines, and adjust for minor physical glitches. The tables list specific recommendations for each of the three training plans and the suggested weekly workouts in each program.

This book is arranged to be read one day at a time, just as you train. Each of the 100 days includes thoughts and tips from me. I hope this weekly minimagazine covering a variety of topics gives you information and inspiration that help complete the training—and eventually the marathon itself.

Some of the writing is mine. But the most important part of the book is what you write yourself. This is the diary page for each day. (See the log sample on page 11.)

I suggest a schedule at the beginning of each week, which you're free to modify as you wish. Tailor it to your needs, list the exact training you plan to do on each of the seven days that follow, and later add the details as you complete the scheduled workout.

Fill in the blanks, and check and circle the options. Match your planned training against what you accomplished. Watch your "physical status" and "psychological status" grades as if they were daily test scores in school. Write yourself a great success story for this marathon.

Day _____

Date _____

Plan _____

Training for the Day

Training Session

Type   Long ____   Fast ____   Easy ____   Other (specify) _____

Distance _____   **Time** _____

Pace _____ **Splits** _____/ _____/ _____/ _____/ _____

Effort   Max ____   Hard ____   Moderate ____   Mild ____   Rest ____

Warm-up _____   **Cool-down** _____

Cross-training (specify) _____

Training Conditions

Location _____   **Time of day** _____

People   Trained alone ____   Trained w/partner ____   Trained w/group ____

Terrain _____   **Surface** _____

Temperature ____   **Humidity** ____   **Wind** ____   **Precipitation** _____

Training Grade for the Day

Physical status   A   B   C   D   F

Psychological status   A   B   C   D   F

Comments _____

_____

_____

TRAINING PLANS

	Cruisers	Pacers	Racers
Runs per week	4 to 5, including 1 big day	5-6, including 1 big day	6 days a week, including 2 big days
Long runs	every 3rd week, longest 18-20 miles	every 2-3 weeks, longest 20-22 miles	2 of 3 weeks, longest 22-24 miles
Half-long	every 3rd week, longest 9-10 miles	every 2-4 weeks, longest 10-11 miles	every 3rd week, longest 11-12 miles
Fast or race	every 3rd week, 5K or less	every 2-4 weeks, 5K to 10K	once a week, 5K to 10K
Easy runs	3-4 days a week, 30-45 minutes	4-5 days a week, 30-60 minutes	4 days a week, 30-60 minutes
Rest days	2-3 a week, cross-training optional	1-2 a week, cross-training optional	1 a week, cross-training optional

Weekly Programs

Training programs appear at the start of each week. Here at a glance is the suggested program for the three groups of marathoners. (* "Week 14" is actually the two-day race weekend.)

CRUISERS

Week	Big Days	Other Runs	Rest Days
1	12-14 miles	3-4 of 30-45 min.	2-3 off
2	6-7 miles	3-4 of 30-45 min.	2-3 off
3	5K race	3-4 of 30-45 min.	2-3 off
4	14-16 miles	3-4 of 30-45 min.	2-3 off
5	7-8 miles	3-4 of 30-45 min.	2-3 off
6	5K race	3-4 of 30-45 min.	2-3 off
7	16-18 miles	3-4 of 30-45 min.	2-3 off
8	8-9 miles	3-4 of 30-45 min.	2-3 off
9	5K race	3-4 of 30-45 min.	2-3 off
10	18-20 miles	3-4 of 30-45 min.	2-3 off
11	9-10 miles	3-4 of 30-45 min.	2-3 off
12	1 hour	3-4 of 30-45 min.	2-3 off
13	none	3-4 of about 30 min.	3-4 off
14*	marathon race	none	1 off
15	none	3-4 short and easy	3-4 off

PACERS

Week	Big Days	Other Runs	Rest Days
1	12-14 miles	4-5 of 30-60 min.	1-2 off
2	6-7 miles	4-5 of 30-60 min.	1-2 off
3	14-16 miles	4-5 of 30-60 min.	1-2 off
4	5K-10K race	4-5 of 30-60 min.	1-2 off
5	16-18 miles	4-5 of 30-60 min.	1-2 off
6	8-9 miles	4-5 of 30-60 min.	1-2 off
7	18-20 miles	4-5 of 30-60 min.	1-2 off
8	5K-10K race	4-5 of 30-60 min.	1-2 off
9	9-10 miles	4-5 of 30-60 min.	1-2 off
10	20-22 miles	4-5 of 30-60 min.	1-2 off
11	5K-10K race	4-5 of 30-60 min.	1-2 off
12	1 hour	4-5 of 30-60 min.	1-2 off
13	none	4-5 of about 30 min.	2-3 off
14*	marathon race	none	1 off
15	none	4-5 short and easy	2-3 off

RACERS

Week	Long Days	Fast Days	Other Runs	Rest Days
1	12-14 miles	1-3 miles	4 of 30-60 min.	1 off
2	14-16 miles	1-3 miles	4 of 30-60 min.	1 off
3	7-8 miles	5K-10K race	4 of 30-60 min.	1 off
4	16-18 miles	1-3 miles	4 of 30-60 min.	1 off
5	18-20 miles	1-3 miles	4 of 30-60 min.	1 off
6	9-10 miles	5K-10K race	4 of 30-60 min.	1 off
7	20-22 miles	1-3 miles	4 of 30-60 min.	1 off
8	21-23 miles	1-3 miles	4 of 30-60 min.	1 off
9	10-11 miles	5K-10K race	4 of 30-60 min.	1 off
10	22-24 miles	1-3 miles	4 of 30-60 min.	1 off
11	11-12 miles	5K-10K race	4 of 30-60 min.	1 off
12	1 hour	1-3 miles	4 of 30-60 min.	1 off
13	none	none	4-6 of about 30 min.	1-3 off
14*	marathon race	none	none	1 off
15	none	none	4-6 short and easy	1-3 off

Age didn't penalize Carla Beurskens. She beat all women at the Honolulu Marathon in her late 30s and on into her 40s.

WEEK ONE:
Starting Now

Your marathon starts now, this week, three months before the event itself. Whatever your starting point or your goal is, you schedule the first long run of this training cycle. It probably is longer than you've run in quite a while—or perhaps ever—so hold down the pace. Remember how much farther you still have to go. Choose your program below, assign workouts to the next seven days' diary pages, and add details there for completed training.

Cruiser Program

Big day: long run of 12 to 14 miles with a mix of running and walking (run no more than 1 mile at a time, and walk for at least one minute). Run-walk this distance no faster than your projected marathon pace.

Other training days: three or four easy runs of 30 to 45 minutes each, with walking breaks optional.

Rest days: two or three with no running, but possibly cross-training.

Pacer Program

Big day: long run of 12 to 14 miles with walking breaks optional (if used, run at least 1 mile and walk no more than one minute). Run this distance about one minute per mile slower than your projected marathon pace.

Other training days: four to five easy runs of 30 to 60 minutes each.

Rest days: one or two with no running, but possibly cross-training.

Racer Program

Long day: 12 to 14 miles. Run about one minute per mile slower than your projected marathon pace.

Fast day: one- to three-mile run at current 10K race pace (this may be broken into shorter intervals that total one to three miles, not counting recovery periods). Warm up and cool down with easy running.

Other training days: four easy runs of 30 to 60 minutes each.

Rest days: one with no running, but possibly cross-training.

Day 1

Thought for the Day

Starting Over

"Let's try again," said Marty Liquori. "That sounded OK, but you didn't answer my question."

Liquori was taping the opening for ESPN's "Running and Racing" segment on the Long Beach Marathon. We stood before the starting line with the final countdown underway, and I'd just blown the first take. The second try was barely more coherent. But time didn't give us another chance.

My worry on the telecast didn't come from standing before a camera, where I'd had lots of practice the last few years. The tension came from starting a marathon for the first time in nine years.

Liquori's first question had begun with "Why?" This launched a garbled explanation of starting over in the marathon. I'd tried to say that marathoners have changed since my first written training advice to them came out in the 1970s. Then most of them were experienced runners. They sought the optimum training needed to qualify for Boston. Now the bulk of marathoners run to finish. Even sped-out runners like me are returning to *run* (even *run-walk)* the distance again, not to race it. My training is more conservative the second time around, and so is my advice to marathoners like me. It deals with the least training we can get by with, and not the most we can do.

No reporter had reason to ask how my Long Beach Marathon went. Nothing distinguished my story from one that thousands of others could tell. Which is to say, to my relief and pleasure, the day went as planned.

Tip for the Day

View the marathon as the Mount Everest of running. It's a peak that every runner dreams of scaling at least once. You too can stand at the top, but not without a long and well-planned climb.

Day 1

Date _____

Plan _____

Training for the Day

Training Session

Type   Long ____   Fast ____   Easy ____   Other (specify) _____

Distance _____   **Time** _____

Pace _____   **Splits** _____ / _____ / _____ / _____ / _____

Effort   Max ____   Hard ____   Moderate ____   Mild ____   Rest ____

Warm-up _____   **Cool-down** _____

Cross-training (specify) _____

Training Conditions

Location _____   **Time of day** _____

People   Trained alone ____   Trained w/partner ____   Trained w/group ____

Terrain _____   **Surface** _____

Temperature ____   **Humidity** ____   **Wind** ____   **Precipitation** _____

Training Grade for the Day

Physical status   A   B   C   D   F

Psychological status   A   B   C   D   F

Comments _____

_____

_____

Day 2

Thought for the Day

The First Time

I took almost 10 years and more than two hundred races to feel ready for my first marathon. And even then, that was the hardest work I had ever done. So I still can't quite believe it when someone says, "I finished a marathon in my first year of running. And it was my first race of any type."

Thousands of people now do it that way. They're almost the majority at the first-timer-friendly New York City, Los Angeles, and Honolulu Marathons.

I'm sure that a marathon is within the reach of most people who are reasonably healthy—if they don't sabotage themselves along the way. Injury, exhaustion, and discouragement are the triple threats to all runners, especially those new to running.

Plans similar to those outlined in this book have proved themselves effective with thousands of beginners, who not only finish their marathon but want to and are able to keep running afterward. I could fill all the remaining pages with examples but will tell you just one story on this page.

An organized marathon training group called the L.A. Road Runners, based in Los Angeles, trains people the right way to go this distance. Nearly all of its members are first-time marathoners, and many are new to running. In one typical year, more than 502 Road Runners started the Los Angeles Marathon. All but two of them finished, and those two—one nursing a knee injury and the other recovering from the flu—probably shouldn't have started that day.

Tip for the Day

Realize that your marathon finish line is nearer than you imagine. If you can race as little as 10 kilometers, you can tack on the remaining 20 miles with a few more months' training.

Day 2

Date _____

Plan _____

Training for the Day

Training Session

Type   Long ____   Fast ____   Easy ____   Other (specify) _____

Distance _____   **Time** _____

Pace _____   **Splits** _____ / _____ / _____ / _____ / _____

Effort   Max ____   Hard ____   Moderate ____   Mild ____   Rest ____

Warm-up _____   **Cool-down** _____

Cross-training (specify) _____

Training Conditions

Location _____   **Time of day** _____

People   Trained alone ____   Trained w/partner ____   Trained w/group ____

Terrain _____   **Surface** _____

Temperature ____   **Humidity** ____   **Wind** ____   **Precipitation** _____

Training Grade for the Day

Physical status	A	B	C	D	F
Psychological status	A	B	C	D	F

Comments _____

_____

_____

Day 3

Thought for the Day

So Much, So Soon

Marathon wannabes are tricky people to deal with. You don't want to put doubts in their head, yet you need to say, "Whoa, what's your hurry?"

Take the case of a 37-year-old named Mark from Washington, D.C., who wrote to me late one December. This clearly was his New Year's resolution letter, though he didn't label it as such. I can't call Mark a runner, because he hadn't yet started to run when he wrote the letter. He was then walking an hour a day, six days a week—but had big plans.

"I want to run the Marine Corps Marathon next fall," he said. In the letter, he outlined a program for the year that first laid some basic running groundwork, then increased his mileage to 60 a week by August, and finally added a two-hour run every weekend of September and October.

Mark asked me if his schedule was too ambitious. I told him it was, and explained that hardly anyone does 60-mile-a-week training anymore. I suggested that Mark revise his plan in these ways:

"First set an initial goal that's shorter term and shorter in length than the marathon, such as running a 10K race. Then if the marathon remains your goal, de-emphasize miles per week and instead concentrate on making the occasional long runs progressively longer and allowing three weeks of recovery in between."

I hate to end this on a down note or to say "told you so," but Mark tried it his way, injured himself, and never reached the marathon he had resolved to run that year. Too much, too soon claimed another victim.

Tip for the Day

Don't think you must turn over your whole life to training. Your long run will become much longer than it has been. But you'll run normally—or even slightly *easier* than usual—the other days.

Day 3

Date _____

Plan _____

Training for the Day

Training Session

Type   Long ____   Fast ____   Easy ____   Other (specify) _____

Distance _____   **Time** _____

Pace _____   **Splits** _____ / _____ / _____ / _____ / _____

Effort   Max ____   Hard ____   Moderate ____   Mild ____   Rest ____

Warm-up _____   **Cool-down** _____

Cross-training (specify) _____

Training Conditions

Location _____   **Time of day** _____

People   Trained alone ____   Trained w/partner ____   Trained w/group ____

Terrain _____   **Surface** _____

Temperature ____   **Humidity** ____   **Wind** ____   **Precipitation** _____

Training Grade for the Day

Physical status   A   B   C   D   F

Psychological status   A   B   C   D   F

Comments _____

_____

_____

Day 4

Thought for the Day

Marathon Mileage

Lots of running advisers circulate marathon schedules nowadays. But few did this in 1977, when my first one ran in *Runner's World*. That article was accidental. An advertiser had dropped out late, leaving a one-page hole to fill with a story. My usual practice back then was to sweat long and hard over stories. The ponderous prose rarely drew any response.

This time, I dashed off the training schedule and a few notes for using it in 20 minutes, and plugged it into the hole. The simple little piece drew more response than anything else I've ever written. I quit counting at 300 letters.

That marathon program enjoyed a long afterlife in article reprints and books. But none of those accurately reflect the training I would now recommend. Most of what I wrote there is obsolete. This doesn't mean it was wrong, because it certainly served many runners well at a time when they had no other way to train.

Now we all know better ways. Thanks to feedback from my marathon-training correspondents and to the teachings of best-selling author Jeff Galloway, my programs shifted in the directions you find here:

- Taking the emphasis away from weekly mileage counts
- Taking longer long runs
- Taking more easy runs and rest days between long runs

You now benefit from 20 years of evolution in marathon theory and practice.

Tip for the Day

Schedule the three elements common to all effective programs: long runs, fast runs, and easy days. Only the amount of each ingredient and the pace of each run differ from runner to runner, and program to program.

Day 4

Date _____

Plan _____

Training for the Day

Training Session

Type   Long ____   Fast ____   Easy ____   Other (specify) _____

Distance _____   **Time** _____

Pace _____   **Splits** _____ / _____ / _____ / _____ / _____

Effort   Max ____   Hard ____   Moderate ____   Mild ____   Rest ____

Warm-up _____   **Cool-down** _____

Cross-training (specify) _____

Training Conditions

Location _____   **Time of day** _____

People   Trained alone ____   Trained w/partner ____   Trained w/group ____

Terrain _____   **Surface** _____

Temperature ____   **Humidity** ____   **Wind** ____   **Precipitation** _____

Training Grade for the Day

Physical status	A	B	C	D	F
Psychological status	A	B	C	D	F

Comments _____

_____

_____

Day 5

Thought for the Day

Now Hear This

Of all the runners I speak to, my favorite groups are marathoners in training. They're on common ground, all headed for the same goal on the same day.

They tremble with enthusiasm and anxiety. They want advice on training and assurance that they're doing it right. They take down every word as if it will spell the difference between their going the distance or not.

I must be careful while talking to them. I need to make clear that what I'm recommending is not necessarily what I'll do myself. "I'm trying to perfect the no-training marathon plan," I tell them only half jokingly. This doesn't mean no *running*, just not much special long-distance work.

My own plan is bare minimum, involving little more than a couple of runs lasting only two hours or so, and these are as much tests (to see if my feet and legs can handle extra distance) as training. I run strictly by time, not distance. I take walking breaks liberally and without guilt.

But I know from talking with thousands of marathoners that most are less experienced and more committed than I am. They want longer long runs than mine. They want to know their training distances. Some want to run every step.

So the program that I *recommend* takes you farther than I'll typically go—by at least 50 percent. It lets you know exactly how long your longest runs are—in miles, not just minutes. It lets you walk or not—your choice.

Tip for the Day

Plan to train far enough to cope with the race distance. This, of course, is your most important concern in preparing for the marathon, since almost no one can run nearly this far without greatly increasing training mileage.

Day 5

Date _____

Plan _____

Training for the Day

Training Session

Type   Long ____   Fast ____   Easy ____   Other (specify) _____

Distance _____   **Time** _____

Pace _____   **Splits** _____ / _____ / _____ / _____ / _____

Effort   Max ____   Hard ____   Moderate ____   Mild ____   Rest ____

Warm-up _____   **Cool-down** _____

Cross-training (specify) _____

Training Conditions

Location _____   **Time of day** _____

People   Trained alone ____   Trained w/partner ____   Trained w/group ____

Terrain _____   **Surface** _____

Temperature ____   **Humidity** ____   **Wind** ____   **Precipitation** _____

Training Grade for the Day

Physical status   A   B   C   D   F

Psychological status   A   B   C   D   F

Comments _____

_____

_____

Day 6

Thought for the Day

Working It Out

Elite runners aren't like you and me. They run faster, of course. But why? (Beyond being younger and more driven, and choosing their parents better.)

That's what I wanted to know while writing my last book, *Road Racers & Their Training.* I surveyed dozens of them to learn what type of work supported their fast running.

First finding: Any two runners can reach similar results from entirely different directions. One might swear by high mileage, another by low but fast miles, and yet they might finish in a dead heat.

Second finding: While individual runners differ enormously in the details of their training, they generally slip into certain traditional patterns. They adopt schedules that satisfy three needs: endurance, speed, and recovery.

To show you what these standard patterns are, I sampled 12 runners. All are Americans, 6 women and 6 men, and most are accomplished marathoners. All are in their 20s and 30s, and all compete internationally. Two have set world records.

As expected, their mileage varies widely. Keith Brantly reports a sample week of 142 miles, while Joan Nesbit ran only 45 in hers. The average of 89 miles a week means little here with a range this broad. But we can see that megamileage isn't the be-all that it was for past generations of elites. Only three of these runners now top 100 miles routinely. The lesson here for you isn't in the numbers but in the fact that weekly mileage is an overrated figure. It's better to focus on big-effort *days* (with enough recovery afterward) than on big-mileage weeks.

Tip for the Day

Plan to train fast enough to handle the marathon's pace (if you are a Pacer concerned with time or a Racer who wants to place well). Pacework includes semi-long runs at marathon tempo or slightly faster.

Day 6

Date _____

Plan _____

Training for the Day

Training Session

Type   Long ____   Fast ____   Easy ____   Other (specify) _____

Distance _____   **Time** _____

Pace _____   **Splits** _____ / _____ / _____ / _____ / _____

Effort   Max ____   Hard ____   Moderate ____   Mild ____   Rest ____

Warm-up _____   **Cool-down** _____

Cross-training (specify) _____

Training Conditions

Location _____   **Time of day** _____

People   Trained alone ____   Trained w/partner ____   Trained w/group ____

Terrain _____   **Surface** _____

Temperature _____   **Humidity** _____   **Wind** _____   **Precipitation** _____

Training Grade for the Day

Physical status	A	B	C	D	F
Psychological status	A	B	C	D	F

Comments _____

_____

_____

Day 7

Thought for the Day

How They Train

Let's look closely at the training of a dozen top American runners, looking for similar patterns in the work that varies greatly in its details:

- A long run starts or ends nearly every week, with Sunday as the preferred day and 15 miles the average distance. Everyone goes at least 10 miles, and several of these runners exceed 20. Half of them take a longish midweek run of 10-plus miles.

- Two-a-day workouts are the norm for all but two of these athletes. (Not coincidentally, the exceptions, Nan Davis and Joan Nesbit, are both mothers of young daughters.) The others average 11+ running sessions per week.

- Speed workouts get everyone's attention. All except Nesbit and Judi St. Hilaire report visiting the track in their sample week. Most of these runners visited the track two times, and many list additional speed-building fartlek workouts, hill repeats, and tempo runs.

- Rest days? Are you kidding! None of these athletes schedule any. The least running anyone lists is 20 minutes. However, everyone alternates harder and easier days, and all pay special attention to tapering for and recovering from races. They define runs of 5 to 10 miles as "easy."

Don't try to adopt all the details of the elites' programs. But marvel at all they do. This training is the foundation of their greatness.

Tip for the Day

Counterbalance the long and fast workouts with easy days. More races are lost by training too long, too fast, or too often, than by running too short, too slow, or too seldom.

Day 7

Date _____

Plan _____

Training for the Day

Training Session

Type   Long ____   Fast ____   Easy ____   Other (specify) _____

Distance _____   **Time** _____

Pace _____ **Splits** _____/ _____/ _____/ _____/ _____

Effort   Max ____   Hard ____   Moderate ____   Mild ____   Rest ____

Warm-up _____   **Cool-down** _____

Cross-training (specify) _____

Training Conditions

Location _____   **Time of day** _____

People   Trained alone ____   Trained w/partner ____   Trained w/group ____

Terrain _____   **Surface** _____

Temperature ____   **Humidity** ____   **Wind** ____   **Precipitation** _____

Training Grade for the Day

Physical status	A	B	C	D	F
Psychological status	A	B	C	D	F

Comments _____

_____

_____

Cosmas Ndeti (No. 1) has been the male runner of the 1990s at the
Boston Marathon, winning three in a row.

WEEK TWO:
Staying Well

Note that one to three days off each week are scheduled for rest, and several others are easy. The number of rest days and type of easy days remain the same throughout your program. They become more important than ever as the hard workouts grow harder. Rest and easy days allow the hard work to *work*. They protect against running yourself into exhaustion and injury. Choose your program below, assign workouts to the next seven days' diary pages, and add details there for completed training.

Cruiser Program
Big day: semi-long run of six to seven miles, or half the distance of last week's long one. Run this distance nonstop, with no walking breaks. Run slightly faster than your projected marathon pace.
Other training days: three or four easy runs of 30 to 45 minutes each, with walking breaks optional.
Rest days: two or three with no running, but possibly cross-training.

Pacer Program
Big day: semi-long run of six to seven miles, or half the distance of last week's long one. Run this distance nonstop, at your projected marathon pace or slightly faster.
Other training days: four to five easy runs of 30 to 60 minutes each.
Rest days: one or two with no running, but possibly cross-training.

Racer Program
Long day: 14 to 16 miles, or about a 2-mile increase from your last one. Run about one minute per mile slower than your projected marathon pace.
Fast day: one- to three-mile run at current 10K race pace (this may be broken into shorter intervals that total one to three miles, not counting recovery periods). Warm up and cool down with easy running.
Other training days: four easy runs of 30 to 60 minutes each.
Rest days: one with no running, but possibly cross-training.

Day 8

Thought for the Day

Getting Hurt

You might think that elite runners don't injure themselves as easily as you do. Training is a process of finding a weak link and a breaking point, and yours arc weaker and lower than theirs.

Both thoughts are half true, I learned from surveying dozens of runners. No, the elites don't hurt as you do; they injure themselves *more often.* And, yes, their breaking points might be higher, but the problems they run into are worse.

Across the running population as a whole, between one-half and two-thirds of us have suffered an injury that halts our training or threatens our careers. Among the elites surveyed, the figure is almost *85 percent.*

Very few of us ever surrender to surgery. But 30 percent of the elites had endured operations and the "Will I ever run again?" doubts that follow. Many had multiple surgeries. Ex-marathon world record holders Jacqueline Hansen and Derek Clayton each report five operations. Many others list repeated injuries of the same type, often on one foot or leg and the same spot on the other side. Janis Klecker, 1992 Olympic Marathon Trial winner, notes six stress fractures, one more than author Joan Ullyot.

Two men blame injuries for effectively ending their careers. Mark Nenow, who still holds the American 10,000 record, says he "never fully recovered" from two hamstring surgeries. Pete Pfitzinger, two-time U.S. Olympic marathoner, said he quit competing when ligament damage refused to heal fully. This is what all runners fear most: the injury that never heals.

Tip for the Day

Never forget that racing—especially at marathon length—is uncomfortable. You can't improve without sometimes venturing into discomfort. But these occasional ventures must be separated by returns to your comfort zone.

Day 8

Date _____

Plan _____

Training for the Day

Training Session

Type   Long _____   Fast _____   Easy _____   Other (specify) _____

Distance _____   **Time** _____

Pace _____   **Splits** _____ / _____ / _____ / _____ / _____

Effort   Max _____   Hard _____   Moderate _____   Mild _____   Rest _____

Warm-up _____   **Cool-down** _____

Cross-training (specify) _____

Training Conditions

Location _____   **Time of day** _____

People   Trained alone _____   Trained w/partner _____   Trained w/group _____

Terrain _____   **Surface** _____

Temperature _____   **Humidity** _____   **Wind** _____   **Precipitation** _____

Training Grade for the Day

Physical status   A   B   C   D   F

Psychological status   A   B   C   D   F

Comments _____

_____

_____

Day 9

Thought for the Day

Getting Better

I find more reasons for hope than despair in the injury reports on elite runners. Most of them recover, many run better than ever after the injury, and some of them learn not to repeat past mistakes.

Derek Clayton had surgeries shortly before and after running the world's first sub-2:10 and then sub-2:09 marathons. Jacqueline Hansen came back from surgery to become the first woman under 2:45 and 2:40. Lorraine Moller had a heel operation before winning her Olympic medal in the marathon.

Yes, Janis Klecker had six stress fractures. But she's had none since 1988. (She won the Olympic Trial Marathon four years later.) And, yes, Joan Ullyot had five of these fractures, among other ailments. But this runner-physician says, "The injuries mainly occurred in the first five to six years, when I was doing too much, too soon."

A few runners never get hurt at all. My survey found that 13 of the 80 have been genetically gifted or smart enough—or just lucky enough—to avoid all injuries. Conservative running doesn't explain their good health. Nor does youthful resilience. Miki Gorman ran ultras before winning the New York City and Boston Marathons in her 40s. Norm Frank, in his mid-60s, had run almost 600 marathons.

The uninjured are a minority within a minority. They're elites whose weak links and breaking points are beyond the reach of their running.

Tip for the Day

Don't swallow the most damaging myth in athletics: *pain equals gain*. No one can stand to train painfully all the time. All you gain from that work is ever-increasing pain—until you can't or won't tolerate it any longer.

Day 9

Date _____

Plan _____

Training for the Day

Training Session

Type   Long ____   Fast ____   Easy ____   Other (specify) _____

Distance _____   **Time** _____

Pace _____   **Splits** _____ / _____ / _____ / _____ / _____

Effort   Max ____   Hard ____   Moderate ____   Mild ____   Rest ____

Warm-up _____   **Cool-down** _____

Cross-training (specify) _____

Training Conditions

Location _____   **Time of day** _____

People   Trained alone ____   Trained w/partner ____   Trained w/group ____

Terrain _____   **Surface** _____

Temperature ____   **Humidity** ____   **Wind** ____   **Precipitation** _____

Training Grade for the Day

Physical status   A   B   C   D   F

Psychological status   A   B   C   D   F

Comments _____

_____

_____

Day 10

Thought for the Day

Try This One

Cosmas Ndeti, the Kenyan who has won three Boston Marathons, won't say much about his training. Most of what he says is meant to hide what he does, not reveal anything. But Mr. Mystery did let a few of his practices slip out in a story reporting his third straight Boston win in 1995. He doesn't just listen to his body but takes its messages as commandments, not just suggestions.

The *New York Times* reported, "He runs according to the way he feels each morning, not according to any rigid schedule. He has been known to wake up, run for a kilometer, then climb back into bed."

Ndeti might call it a day after a single K; but for those of us who measure runs by miles, a sound check at one mile will work just as well.

"Listen to your body," all the advisers say. But they rarely explain *when* to listen closest. Before the run isn't the right time. That's when the body tells the biggest lies—trying to convince you that it feels better or worse than it really does.

Running injuries often hibernate between runs. You might feel, "I'm OK," while planning the day's training, then try to run as planned after the injury flares up again and you need to rest it. Just as often, you stiffen up between runs. You might think before starting, "I'm hurting and better take the day off," when all you need is a warm-up.

A brief run sorts out these feelings. One little mile restores honesty, so plan just to run that first mile. *Then* listen to your body, and only then choose what it will let you do next.

Tip for the Day

Think of the marathon as an unnatural act. Exciting and challenging as this race (as well as training that mimics it) might be, it tears you down, and you must build back up after each hard effort with many easier ones.

Day 10

Date _____

Plan _____

Training for the Day

Training Session

Type   Long ____   Fast ____   Easy ____   Other (specify) _____

Distance _____   **Time** _____

Pace _____   **Splits** _____ / _____ / _____ / _____ / _____

Effort   Max ____   Hard ____   Moderate ____   Mild ____   Rest ____

Warm-up _____   **Cool-down** _____

Cross-training (specify) _____

Training Conditions

Location _____   **Time of day** _____

People   Trained alone ____   Trained w/partner ____   Trained w/group ____

Terrain _____   **Surface** _____

Temperature ____   **Humidity** ____   **Wind** ____   **Precipitation** _____

Training Grade for the Day

Physical status   A   B   C   D   F

Psychological status   A   B   C   D   F

Comments ____ _____

_____

_____

Day 11

Thought for the Day

Miles Don't Count

While speaking to a group of marathoners in training, I made a pitch for resting. "When you're taking longer long runs for a marathon," I said, "you probably need an extra rest day each week to compensate."

During question time, a woman from the audience said, "I see your point about days off. But I'm afraid to take any because they hurt my weekly mileage." My answer: "I don't just want to hurt it. I'd like to help *kill* it." It's the mile counting that hurts. To stop the hurting, we have to quit keeping score this way.

The damage takes many forms, from subtle to serious. At the least, your program flattens to doing the same distance every day as the simplest way to meet the weekly quota. You avoid the lows by skipping the highs.

You sacrifice speedwork and short races because they would cut into your distance that day. Or you add a few meaningless miles in a second session each day to inflate the total. Or at worst, you refuse to take the "penalty" of what you may need most: a day off. Mile counting pressures you to run too much on days when you need less. Then it leaves you too tired or sore to run enough on days when you need more running.

I'm not antidistance. In fact, I emphasize it more than ever. Only now the emphasis is better placed: on an occasional high-mileage *day*, not on more miles per week. The program in this book contains longer long runs than previous versions of my marathon schedule, but also shorter short ones and more days of nothing.

Tip for the Day

Alternate hard and easy days only if you are an elite athlete. Most runners are slower to rebound from hard days, and one big session each *week* is about all the midpack finisher can tolerate.

Day 11

Date _____

Plan _____

Training for the Day

Training Session

Type   Long ____   Fast ____   Easy ____   Other (specify) _____

Distance _____   **Time** _____

Pace _____   **Splits** _____ / _____ / _____ / _____ / _____

Effort   Max ____   Hard ____   Moderate ____   Mild ____   Rest ____

Warm-up _____   **Cool-down** _____

Cross-training (specify) _____

Training Conditions

Location _____   **Time of day** _____

People   Trained alone ____   Trained w/partner ____   Trained w/group ____

Terrain _____   **Surface** _____

Temperature _____   **Humidity** _____   **Wind** _____   **Precipitation** _____

Training Grade for the Day

Physical status	A	B	C	D	F
Psychological status	A	B	C	D	F

Comments _____

_____

_____

Day 12

Thought for the Day

Rest Assured

Rest isn't just for the weak of will and body anymore. It isn't just for the older runners whose recovery has slowed. Rest is as big a part of the training puzzle as long runs and speedwork. For everyone.

I say this as a born-again rester. But don't just take my word for it. Read the testimonials of a much higher level of believers, appearing in the January 1995 issue of *Runner's World.* Dave Kuehls asked 17 runners about their resolutions for the new year. Six of them vowed to get more rest. Two of these runners are Olympic gold medalists, and another has held world records. Their comments:

Joan Samuelson: "I'm finally going to take a tip from something my older brother told me several years ago: 'Rest is the basis of all activity.' "

Frank Shorter: "As soon as any pain inhibits my biomechanics, I'll go immediately to cross-training for two weeks. I won't run at all."

Arturo Barrios: "I won't overrace. . . . I'll give myself time to recover after hard races, taking at least five weeks off from racing after a marathon."

A young Alberto Salazar was one of the hardest training, biggest winning, and most injured runners in U.S. history. Hindsight now tells him that his biggest mistake was not recovering enough after races. He now applies this lesson to his own running and passes it on to the athletes he coaches: Rest is not a four-letter word.

Tip for the Day

Recover actively, if you wish. Recovery doesn't require complete rest (although at least one day off a week comes highly recommended). You can recover while still satisfying the urge to run by running easily.

Day 12

Date _____

Plan _____

Training for the Day

Training Session

Type   Long ____   Fast ____   Easy ____   Other (specify) _____

Distance _____   **Time** _____

Pace _____   **Splits** _____ / _____ / _____ / _____ / _____

Effort   Max ____   Hard ____   Moderate ____   Mild ____   Rest ____

Warm-up _____   **Cool-down** _____

Cross-training (specify) _____

Training Conditions

Location _____   **Time of day** _____

People   Trained alone ____   Trained w/partner ____   Trained w/group ____

Terrain _____   **Surface** _____

Temperature ____   **Humidity** ____   **Wind** ____   **Precipitation** _____

Training Grade for the Day

Physical status   A   B   C   D   F

Psychological status   A   B   C   D   F

Comments _____

_____

_____

Day 13

Thought for the Day

Rest of the Story

Gerry Lindgren was a prodigy, making an Olympic team at 18 and setting a world record at 19. He also was and is a leg-puller who exaggerates for shock value. When *Honolulu Advertiser* writer Mike Tymn asked about reports that he put in 200-mile weeks, Gerry said, "Well, actually I was doing 350 a week for a time."

That would require averaging 50 miles a day. The figure is suspect, but there's no disputing that Lindgren worked harder than anyone so young in his or maybe any other generation.

"Back then [the 1960s], nobody ran long," he told Tymn. "I guess I was too stupid to know that I shouldn't do that much. If I could go back and do it all over again, I think I'd take more time off before big races. The only time I set records was right after an injury, within a week or so of coming back. I can look back and think, golly, if I was doing that good after I'd been injured, it must be because I was resting."

Runners need to see what our illustrious ancestors couldn't. But we also need to know that rest has its limits. Cosmas Ndeti, who set a course record at the 1994 Boston Marathon, exceeded those limits. Jere Longman reported in the *New York Times* that "from late April until August, Ndeti didn't run a mile in training. Not one. He lounged around and put on 16 pounds."

Ndeti told the reporter, "My body needed rest and food." It also needed more training than he could do in two months. The Kenyan didn't get past 20 miles at the Chicago Marathon in October.

Running and resting are teammates. They only work together.

Tip for the Day

Stay well within the comfort zone on easy days. For experienced runners, this might mean comfortably paced runs of up to an hour. Newer marathoners shouldn't feel guilty about doing as little as a half hour.

Day 13

Date _____

Plan _____

Training for the Day

Training Session

Type   Long ____   Fast ____   Easy ____   Other (specify) _____

Distance _____   **Time** _____

Pace _____   **Splits** _____ / _____ / _____ / _____ / _____

Effort   Max ____   Hard ____   Moderate ____   Mild ____   Rest ____

Warm-up _____   **Cool-down** _____

Cross-training (specify) _____

Training Conditions

Location _____   **Time of day** _____

People   Trained alone ____   Trained w/partner ____   Trained w/group ____

Terrain _____   **Surface** _____

Temperature ____   **Humidity** ____   **Wind** ____   **Precipitation** _____

Training Grade for the Day

Physical status   A   B   C   D   F

Psychological status   A   B   C   D   F

Comments _____

_____

_____

Day 14

Thought for the Day

No Hurry, No Worry

Meyer Friedman, MD, coined the phrase "Type-A personality." He identified its main symptom as "hurry sickness." Dr. Friedman listed its traits as "excessive competitive drive, aggressiveness, impatience, and a harrying sense of time urgency."

Runners are particularly susceptible to this affliction, because our sport is custom-made for hurriers. It always holds up new times to beat and deadlines to meet.

But if time is the cause of hurry sickness, it can also supply the cure. We can work at relaxing by making friends with the clock. One of the best changes I ever made to my running was switching to the time standard. I quit counting miles and simply ran for, say, an hour without knowing the distance covered.

I began running this way for a practical reason: not wanting to measure all courses and to run only these routes.

Our natural urge when running by miles is to finish them quickly. Running by minutes, which can't be rushed, we naturally adopt a less hurried pace.

But another problem can remain, even with time running. That's scheduling the running time too tightly—rushing to get started, hurrying away afterward, and canceling the calming effect of the run itself.

The cure: Take more time than needed. Provide a relaxed buffer period on either side of the run by setting aside twice as much time as the run requires. Make friends with the clock.

Tip for the Day

Treat the easy runs as the meat and potatoes (or beans and rice, if you're vegetarian) of the running diet. The dessert comes as small, infrequent portions of racing and training at abnormal distances and speeds.

Day 14

Date _____

Plan _____

Training for the Day

Training Session

Type   Long ____   Fast ____   Easy ____   Other (specify) _____

Distance _____   **Time** _____

Pace _____   **Splits** _____ / _____ / _____ / _____ / _____

Effort   Max ____   Hard ____   Moderate ____   Mild ____   Rest ____

Warm-up _____   **Cool-down** _____

Cross-training (specify) _____

Training Conditions

Location _____   **Time of day** _____

People   Trained alone ____   Trained w/partner ____   Trained w/group ____

Terrain _____   **Surface** _____

Temperature ____   **Humidity** ____   **Wind** ____   **Precipitation** _____

Training Grade for the Day

Physical status   A   B   C   D   F

Psychological status   A   B   C   D   F

Comments _____

_____

_____

Women and men run side by side, stride for stride in most marathons.
This pair paces each other at Napa Valley.

WEEK THREE:
Going Long

This week's Thoughts and Tips deal entirely with running long. So let's take a few moments here to consider the flip side of longer running, which is not running at all. On nonrun days, you don't need total rest but only a break from the pounding of running. You can cross-train on some or all of those days—with biking, swimming, running in water, and walking being your best alternatives. Choose your program below, assign workouts to the next seven days' diary pages, and add details there for completed training.

Cruiser Program
Big day: race of five kilometers, or fast solo run of one to three miles. In all cases, run at least one minute per mile faster than your projected marathon pace.
Other training days: three or four easy runs of 30 to 45 minutes each, with walking breaks optional.
Rest days: two or three with no running, but possibly cross-training.

Pacer Program
Big day: long run of 14 to 16 miles, or about a 2-mile increase from your last one. Walking breaks optional. Run about one minute per mile slower than your projected marathon pace.
Other training days: four to five easy runs of 30 to 60 minutes each.
Rest days: one or two with no running, but possibly cross-training.

Racer Program
Long day: semi-long run of seven to eight miles, or half the distance of last week's long one. Run at your projected marathon pace or slightly faster.
Fast day: race of 5K to 10K, or one- to three-mile run at current 10K race pace (this may be broken into shorter intervals that total one to three miles, not counting recovery periods). Warm up and cool down with easy running.
Other training days: four easy runs of 30 to 60 minutes each.
Rest days: one with no running, but possibly cross-training.

Day 15

Thought for the Day

In Defense of Distance

The two writers are well-meaning supporters of the sport. So I won't mention them by name to spare them any embarrassment. I'll just say that they both ride the wave of conservatism now sweeping the sport. It tugs runners down toward safe minimums in length and frequency of runs.

The first writer referred to the foremost authority on stress: "Hans Selye tells us that one has only so much reserve, and when one goes to the well too often the reserve is gone—permanently." This writer then disparaged the efforts of hard-training marathoners.

The second writer referred to the foremost authority on running physiology by saying, "David Costill has research to prove that beyond 50 miles a week you lose anaerobic strength. In effect, you decrease your maximum speed." This writer boasted of his own 30-mile-a-week training.

They tell us to run less distance, run less often, and don't run many—if any—marathons. They may be right in what they say, but wrong in what this implies: runners should never push their limits, never take chances, never risk making mistakes.

At certain times, I've gone to all the extremes—including the distance of long runs and total weekly mileage. I've paid for these excesses but never regretted them. They were all part of the adventure. The highs made the running worth doing and the lows tolerable.

I haven't forgotten where I came from. That's why I'm slow to criticize any runner who tries to go great distances.

Tip for the Day

Focus your training program on the long run, which far exceeds everyday training distance. The frequency and maximum length will vary according to your goals, but long runs are equally important for everyone.

Day 15

Date _____

Plan _____

Training for the Day

Training Session

Type   Long ____   Fast ____   Easy ____   Other (specify) _____

Distance _____   **Time** _____

Pace _____   **Splits** _____ / _____ / _____ / _____ / _____

Effort   Max ____   Hard ____   Moderate ____   Mild ____   Rest ____

Warm-up _____   **Cool-down** _____

Cross-training (specify) _____

Training Conditions

Location _____   **Time of day** _____

People   Trained alone ____   Trained w/partner ____   Trained w/group ____

Terrain _____   **Surface** _____

Temperature ____   **Humidity** ____   **Wind** ____   **Precipitation** _____

Training Grade for the Day

Physical status   A   B   C   D   F

Psychological status   A   B   C   D   F

Comments _____

_____

_____

Day 16

Thought for the Day

Trash Burners

A disparaging term sometimes applied to long runs is "garbage miles." Sure they are—in the best possible sense. They burn off unwanted weight and fat.

One of my earliest articles dealt with Peter Snell, Olympic triple gold medalist in the 1960s who ran then-unheard-of mileage for a miler. He trained more than most *marathoners* of his era. "One reason this worked so well for him might have been that he was heavy," I wrote. "He gained weight easily if he wasn't training a lot. His 100-mile weeks gave him his raw-boned look."

Mike Tymn, a *National Masters News* columnist and top runner himself, called one of his workouts a "calorie burner." It was extra long and extra slow. Tymn wrote, "For those of us who like our ice cream and chocolate chip cookies, and find it increasingly difficult to shed excess weight, the CB serves as a purpose beyond training for a race."

Long runs are fat burners in ways you can see in a mirror and on the scales. They also teach you to burn fat in ways you can feel.

Fat isn't all bad. The stored fat in the body is a fuel. (But lest you think more is better, realize that a pound or so would fuel a marathon.)

In shorter runs and early in the long ones, you burn mostly carbohydrate-based fuels. But the body gradually switches to burning fat as the distance increases. One of the great benefits of long runs is training your fat-burning mechanism to kick in efficiently. This only happens with hours of running.

Tip for the Day

With the marathon in sight, you've already started adding distance to your long run. Now ask yourself: How much farther do I need to go, and how can I go that far without running into trouble?

Day 16

Date _____

Plan _____

Training for the Day

Training Session

Type   Long ____   Fast ____   Easy ____   Other (specify) _____

Distance _____   **Time** _____

Pace _____   **Splits** _____ / _____ / _____ / _____ / _____

Effort   Max ____   Hard ____   Moderate ____   Mild ____   Rest ____

Warm-up _____   **Cool-down** _____

Cross-training (specify) _____

Training Conditions

Location _____   **Time of day** _____

People   Trained alone ____   Trained w/partner ____   Trained w/group ____

Terrain _____   **Surface** _____

Temperature ____   **Humidity** ____   **Wind** ____   **Precipitation** _____

Training Grade for the Day

Physical status   A   B   C   D   F

Psychological status   A   B   C   D   F

Comments _____

_____

_____

Day 17

Thought for the Day

So Long

When Human Kinetics asked me to write this book about marathon training, my first thought was: Before writing about it, maybe I need to *do* it. What I'd done lately hardly qualified as training.

To train is to do something extraordinary as preparation for a special race. I'd gone beyond my ordinary one-hour limit only a few times a year, and even then hadn't "trained" more than half the marathon distance.

I've never wanted to see how much work I could stand, but how little I could get away with. I'd tried to perfect the no-training marathon program, facing each of the past several events with less homework than the last. Before the latest one, I'd hit an all-time low: just a pair of two-hour runs in the previous two months. That wasn't enough.

The marathon time was slow, but not abnormally so. I can live with slowness if the marathon goes well otherwise. This one didn't. My undertrained legs shuffled stiffly through the final hour. The rundown feeling reminded me that you can't fake a marathon. You can get a lot from a little training, but you can't get something for nothing. And I'd done next to nothing. The only special training had been long runs, but these had come too seldom and had been too short.

So my needs are simple: a few more long runs at slightly longer distances. Nothing extreme, but enough to satisfy the minimum training requirements that I'm asking you to meet.

Tip for the Day

Aim to run at least two-thirds of the marathon distance (at least 17 miles) before raceday. Three-fourths (20 miles) or more is an even better goal, since each extra mile beyond the minimum adds assurance of finishing.

Day 17

Date _____

Plan _____

Training for the Day

Training Session

Type   Long ____   Fast ____   Easy ____   Other (specify) _____

Distance _____   **Time** _____

Pace _____   **Splits** _____ / _____ / _____ / _____ / _____

Effort   Max ____   Hard ____   Moderate ____   Mild ____   Rest ____

Warm-up _____   **Cool-down** _____

Cross-training (specify) _____

Training Conditions

Location _____   **Time of day** _____

People   Trained alone ____   Trained w/partner ____   Trained w/group ____

Terrain _____   **Surface** _____

Temperature ____   **Humidity** ____   **Wind** ____   **Precipitation** _____

Training Grade for the Day

Physical status   A   B   C   D   F

Psychological status   A   B   C   D   F

Comments _____

_____

_____

Day 18

Thought for the Day

Long Enough

When my maximum long runs of a half-marathon revealed themselves as inadequate marathon training, the next question became: What's long enough?

I certainly wouldn't go to Jeff Galloway lengths. I think the world of Jeff and applaud him for attracting legions of followers to his marathon program. But I'm not prepared to go to the great lengths that they are.

"You will hit the wall at exactly the length of your longest run," he says. "So you need to work up to 26 miles in training." Jeff adds important qualifiers that often go unheard or unheeded: Hold down the pace, and take regular walking breaks. Using these tricks in training eases the effort and speeds the recovery.

The easiest solution would be to follow Jeff Galloway and train up to full marathon distance. But I balk at that for reasons both personal and philosophical. The first reason is pure laziness. Only the hoopla of the race can move me to run anywhere near 26 miles. The second reason rationalizes the first. Training all of it would rob the marathon of its mystery. I like to leave the late miles as questions to answer only on the big day.

So how much training is enough? If half-marathon runs are too short and full marathons seem too long, simply split the difference. Run at least three-fourths of a marathon in practice. Then trust the raceday magic to take care of the last quarter.

Tip for the Day

Take your long runs as much as one minute per mile slower than projected marathon pace. At faster paces, these runs become too much like the race itself—and require long recovery periods that interrupt regular training.

Day 18

Date _____

Plan _____

Training for the Day

Training Session

Type   Long ____   Fast ____   Easy ____   Other (specify) _____

Distance _____   **Time** _____

Pace _____   **Splits** _____ / _____ / _____ / _____ / _____

Effort   Max ____   Hard ____   Moderate ____   Mild ____   Rest ____

Warm-up _____   **Cool-down** _____

Cross-training (specify) _____

Training Conditions

Location _____   **Time of day** _____

People   Trained alone ____   Trained w/partner ____   Trained w/group ____

Terrain _____   **Surface** _____

Temperature ____   **Humidity** ____   **Wind** ____   **Precipitation** _____

Training Grade for the Day

Physical status   A   B   C   D   F

Psychological status   A   B   C   D   F

Comments _____

_____

_____

Day 19

Thought for the Day

Minutes and Miles

Love what I write or hate it, agree with it or disagree. You buy that right with your magazine subscription or purchase of a book, and I can live with any of those verdicts.

The only reaction that truly bothers me is confusion. When a reader's reply starts with, "I don't understand . . ." that means I've slipped up as a writer—and not by saying something wrong but by leaving something out.

Two of my pet themes confused Jim Bride of Beaverton, Oregon, when he read the book *Better Runs.* "The first question relates to measuring runs by time rather than by miles," wrote Bride. "I was curious as to whether or not you worried about tracking the effort that you expended during the run." He went on to say that time without distance didn't tell him much. "A 50-minute run could be an easy six-mile or a hard nine-mile. Gauging effort is important to me, and I can't do that when I run strictly by time—or while running by miles without timing them."

Bride is right. Time running doesn't account for effort. In fact, it eases the effort, because you can't make time pass faster by rushing. You naturally back off. That's exactly what many runners need to do—make their "easy" runs easier. On the other hand, everyone sometimes needs a push, as well as the certainty of running a known distance in a known time.

In *Marathon Training*, I recommend giving the running a split personality. That is, take the important runs—long ones, tempo runs, speed workouts—by timed distance and the easy ones by time only.

Tip for the Day

Increase the length of your long runs by about two miles each time. This gives a sense of progress without overwhelming your ability to take each of the new steps at one- to three-week intervals.

Day 19

Date _____

Plan _____

Training for the Day

Training Session

Type   Long _____   Fast _____   Easy _____   Other (specify) _____

Distance _____   **Time** _____

Pace _____   **Splits** _____ / _____ / _____ / _____ / _____

Effort   Max _____   Hard _____   Moderate _____   Mild _____   Rest _____

Warm-up _____   **Cool-down** _____

Cross-training (specify) _____

Training Conditions

Location _____   **Time of day** _____

People   Trained alone _____   Trained w/partner _____   Trained w/group _____

Terrain _____   **Surface** _____

Temperature _____   **Humidity** _____   **Wind** _____   **Precipitation** _____

Training Grade for the Day

Physical status   A   B   C   D   F

Psychological status   A   B   C   D   F

Comments _____

_____

_____

Day 20

Thought for the Day

Long May They Run

Reviews are mixed for long runs. Some runners love them, some hate them, but they all take them.

Derek Clayton, who set two world marathon records in the 1960s, says bluntly, "I hated the Saturday 24-miler because it was so tough, especially on top of a hard week. But it was invaluable preparation for a fast marathon, and in my opinion still is."

Kathrine Switzer, an early New York City Marathon winner, names the long Sunday run as her favorite. "It always was, and still is," she says. "The race is first about being able to cover the distance, no matter what. The long run always gave me physical and mental strength. Later in life, this translated to always being able to last it out in other circumstances."

We can loosely define the "long run" as one at least twice the length of any other. It's a weekend ritual for most runners and the centerpiece of marathon training.

I asked about this practice when questioning dozens of athletes for the book *Road Racers & Their Training*. Since this run is the longest and most critical for marathoners, I focus now on how far 10 of them ran.

The women ran between 2:29:27 and 2:38:19 (which was a world record when Jacqueline Hansen ran it in 1975). The men ran 2:12:26 down to 2:08:34 (Derek Clayton's long-standing world record). The one common element in their otherwise widely varying training: a regular long run averaging at least as much time as their marathon would require.

Tip for the Day

Reach maximum training distance in the 10th week of this program. This gives you three weeks to recover before the marathon, which assures you that you'll go into the race healthy, fresh, and eager.

Day 20

Date _____

Plan _____

Training for the Day

Training Session

Type   Long ____   Fast ____   Easy ____   Other (specify) _____

Distance _____   **Time** _____

Pace _____   **Splits** _____ / _____ / _____ / _____ / _____

Effort   Max ____   Hard ____   Moderate ____   Mild ____   Rest ____

Warm-up _____   **Cool-down** _____

Cross-training (specify) _____

Training Conditions

Location _____   **Time of day** _____

People   Trained alone ____   Trained w/partner ____   Trained w/group ____

Terrain _____   **Surface** _____

Temperature ____   **Humidity** ____   **Wind** ____   **Precipitation** _____

Training Grade for the Day

Physical status   A   B   C   D   F

Psychological status   A   B   C   D   F

Comments _____

_____

_____

Day 21

Thought for the Day

Long-Run Solutions

Ten top runners told me exactly how far their longest run took them in peak training, three to six weeks before their best race. They averaged 23 miles, and all ran at least 20 miles.

Kenny Moore reached 30 miles shortly before his fourth-place finish at the Munich Olympics, and Ron Hill went 28 miles before becoming the second runner ever to break 2:10. But from this group, only these two men exceeded marathon distance in training.

Only a handful of these runners noted their pace, and they all trained well below race tempo. Derek Clayton, a renowned pace pusher, trained long at about 5:50 per mile but raced a minute faster. Moore's 30-miler passed at 6:05 pace, while he ran 5:00-flat miles in marathons. This spread is common among the marathoners I surveyed.

Most of them either ran their miles without recording the time, or ran for a time period without listing the distance. Time runners Nancy Ditz and Jacqueline Gareau went 2-1/2 hours on their longest runs, which was exactly how long their best marathons lasted.

Getting used to lasting the full time of the race might be the most important factor in going long. Pete Pfitzinger trained for marathon-like time periods on 22-mile runs. "The long run over hills, starting moderately [6:10 pace in his case] and finishing hard [5:30 miles] builds mental and physical toughness for the marathon," says Pfitzinger. "These runs enabled me to run the second half of the marathon within one minute of the first half and to finish strong." Pfitzinger twice finished strongly enough to lead American marathoners at the Olympics.

Tip for the Day

View each of your long runs as a dress rehearsal of the marathon. Run on the race course if possible, or at least mimic its terrain. Test the shoes and clothing you'll wear on raceday, and the foods and drinks you'll take.

Day 21

Date _____

Plan _____

Training for the Day

Training Session

Type   Long ____   Fast ____   Easy ____   Other (specify) _____

Distance _____   **Time** _____

Pace _____   **Splits** _____ / _____ / _____ / _____ / _____

Effort   Max ____   Hard ____   Moderate ____   Mild ____   Rest ____

Warm-up _____   **Cool-down** _____

Cross-training (specify) _____   _____

Training Conditions

Location _____   **Time of day** _____

People   Trained alone ____   Trained w/partner ____   Trained w/group ____

Terrain _____   **Surface** _____

Temperature ____   **Humidity** ____   **Wind** ____   **Precipitation** _____

Training Grade for the Day

Physical status   A   B   C   D   F

Psychological status   A   B   C   D   F

Comments _____

_____

_____

The most famous final stretch in the running world: Boylston Street in Boston, where the marathon has ended since 1897.

WEEK FOUR:
Taking Breaks

Walking breaks are standard in the Cruiser program, but they can help Pacers and even Racers who might be having trouble extending their long runs or recovering quickly from them. The recommended mix: run about a mile, then walk about a minute before running again. Think of this as interval training for long distances. Choose your program below, assign workouts to the next seven days' diary pages, and add details there for completed training.

Cruiser Program
Big day: long run of 14 to 16 miles, or about a 2-mile increase from your last one. Mix running and walking while covering the distance no faster than your projected marathon pace.
Other training days: three or four easy runs of 30 to 45 minutes each, with walking breaks optional.
Rest days: two or three with no running, but possibly cross-training.

Pacer Program
Big day: race of 5K to 10K, or fast solo run of one to three miles (may be broken into intervals) at current 10K race pace. Warm up and cool down with easy running.
Other training days: four to five easy runs of 30 to 60 minutes each.
Rest days: one or two with no running, but possibly cross-training.

Racer Program
Long day: long run of 16 to 18 miles, or about a 2-mile increase from the last one. Run about one minute per mile slower than marathon pace.
Fast day: one- to three-mile run at current 10K race pace (this may be broken into shorter intervals that total one to three miles, not counting recovery periods). Warm up and cool down with easy running.
Other training days: four easy runs of 30 to 60 minutes each.
Rest days: one with no running, but possibly cross-training.

Day 22

Thought for the Day

Cruise Control

Jeff Galloway is one persuasive guy. I never fail to bring home something useful from my annual visit to his running camp at Squaw Valley. One year, he taught me to take days off. Another, he led me back into marathons. Yet another, he showed me the value of running two days before resting. Last year, he convinced me that eating PowerBars during marathons would solve my late-race fuel crisis.

The latest lesson didn't come from anything Jeff said but from his book *Return of the Tribes*. A major theme is "cruisin'." He writes it that way, with the apostrophe.

Cruisin' is how we're designed to cover long distances on foot, he explains. By mixing slow running and walking breaks, we can go almost indefinitely. Cruisin' is now a standard feature of his marathon program, which has thousands of followers. I believed in it even before Jeff gave it a name and legitimacy.

Now he has made a believer of me as he never intended. Ever since I voluntarily started taking days off, I've had one remaining problem: What to do on the runless days? Swim? Impractical. I would take more time getting to and from the pool than I'd spend in it. Bike? Uncomfortable. This is a dark, cold, and wet activity for most of the year at the hour I prefer to go out. Weights? Unsuitable. They don't in any way mimic the feel of running.

Jeff's choice: Cruise in reverse by adding *running* breaks to a walk.

Tip for the Day

If the distances and progress rates quoted for long runs sound imposing, ease the mileage by adopting the technique of intermittent running. For each mile you run, stop and walk for about a minute.

Day 22

Date _____

Plan _____

Training for the Day

Training Session

Type Long ____ Fast ____ Easy ____ Other (specify) _____

Distance _____ **Time** _____

Pace _____ **Splits** _____ / _____ / _____ / _____ / _____

Effort Max ____ Hard ____ Moderate ____ Mild ____ Rest ____

Warm-up _____ **Cool-down** _____

Cross-training (specify) _____

Training Conditions

Location _____ **Time of day** _____

People Trained alone ____ Trained w/partner ____ Trained w/group ____

Terrain _____ **Surface** _____

Temperature ____ **Humidity** ____ **Wind** ____ **Precipitation** _____

Training Grade for the Day

Physical status   A   B   C   D   F

Psychological status   A   B   C   D   F

Comments _____

_____

_____

Day 23

Thought for the Day

Cruisin' in Reverse

Doing nothing on the "rest" days left too big a hole in my day. So I dressed as if to run, went out at the same time, for the same period of time, and to the same places I'd go to run. Except I didn't run. I walked instead.

This was a good substitute. But Jeff Galloway offered a better one, a variation of his cruisin' theme. After coming back from Jeff's running camp, I tinkered with cruisin' in reverse—by flip-flopping the running and walking ratios.

Like most good changes in my routine, this one slipped in unannounced. I didn't plot it first, then test it. One day, it just popped up. A running break of about a minute appeared in the day's walk, then another minirun, then a couple more in what is still basically a walk on a rest day.

So what's the plan? My instinctive changes always grow into plans. Go 30 to 60 minutes, the normal range of running time on an easy day. Run easily for about a minute (untimed, just as walking spells are estimated during long runs), and space these runs widely with walks (just as the walks are spaced within runs). Stop at the first hints of pain or fatigue, which might interfere with the next run.

The only problem left is what to call this mix. I can't use Jeff Galloway's word "cruisin'," since it describes something different. How about plain old "walking"? This isn't purely a walk anymore, but neither is what I call a run purely running. The line between the two activities blurs more all the time. And all of my days are better for that.

Tip for the Day

Look at the payoffs: You can instantly double the length of your longest nonstop running distance by adding walking breaks. You can also maintain a faster pace for the running portions and recover quicker.

Day 23

Date _____

Plan _____

Training for the Day

Training Session

Type   Long ____   Fast ____   Easy ____   Other (specify) _____

Distance _____   **Time** _____

Pace _____   **Splits** _____ / _____ / _____ / _____ / _____

Effort   Max ____   Hard ____   Moderate ____   Mild ____   Rest ____

Warm-up _____   **Cool-down** _____

Cross-training (specify) _____

Training Conditions

Location _____   **Time of day** _____

People   Trained alone ____   Trained w/partner ____   Trained w/group ____

Terrain _____   **Surface** _____

Temperature ____   **Humidity** ____   **Wind** ____   **Precipitation** _____

Training Grade for the Day

Physical status   A   B   C   D   F

Psychological status   A   B   C   D   F

Comments _____

_____

_____

Day 24

Thought for the Day

Cathy the Cruiser

Cathy Troisi of Seneca Falls, New York, only began running in 1994. "Before that," she says, "I had 2-1/2 years of daily walking under my soles, to the tune of two-thousand-plus miles annually."

She isn't so much a runner now as someone Jeff Galloway calls a cruiser who mixes running and walking. Cathy is a crusader as well. Most of her efforts go into raising money for cancer patients. She directs an event in her hometown with that goal, and does marathons for that purpose. Before adding running, she walked her marathons in about 6-1/2 to 7 hours.

Then came her fateful decision to sign up for a Galloway camp. Says Cathy, "I went off to my first camp experience with some trepidation. Would I be the oldest? Would I be the slowest? Although I was close on both counts, I was neither."

Galloway introduced her to cruisin'. Her preferred mix became run six minutes, walk one minute. "Somewhere along the way, I dubbed this 'intervals'," she says. "That fall, I did my first interval marathon in 4:48." This put her about two hours ahead of walk-only pace. Cathy entered Boston as a fund-raiser the next spring, shaving another 10 minutes from her PR.

Maybe she could have done all this by running steadily. But she wouldn't care to try. "The most I've ever run without intervals is six miles," she says. "I consider myself a recreational runner. I do my runs/walks mainly for fund-raising, and the same amount of money is raised whether I walk, run, or 'interval'."

Tip for the Day

If you don't like the word "walk," think of it as another application of interval training. Intervals break a large chunk of work into smaller pieces to make the total workload more manageable.

Day 24

Date _____

Plan _____

Training for the Day

Training Session

Type   Long ____   Fast ____   Easy ____   Other (specify) _____

Distance _____ **Time** _____

Pace _____ **Splits** _____ / _____ / _____ / _____ / _____

Effort   Max ____   Hard ____   Moderate ____   Mild ____   Rest ____

Warm-up _____ **Cool-down** _____

Cross-training (specify) _____

Training Conditions

Location _____ **Time of day** _____

People   Trained alone ____   Trained w/partner ____   Trained w/group ____

Terrain _____ **Surface** _____

Temperature ____ **Humidity** ____ **Wind** ____ **Precipitation** _____

Training Grade for the Day

Physical status   A   B   C   D   F

Psychological status   A   B   C   D   F

Comments _____

_____

_____

Day 25

Thought for the Day

Running Out of Time

Make no mistake about how I view Tom Derderian. Before questioning a few paragraphs he wrote, let me praise all he has done.

His *Boston Marathon* history book is one of the biggest (at 664 pages) and best ever written on running. His columns in *New England Runner* magazine combine bite with humor. It's hard to debate someone who has done so much, so well. But I can't let a column of his pass without a rebuttal.

"Call me an elitist if you like," Tom wrote, "but I settle in with the old school of marathon officials. Four hours after the race started, the old officials clicked off their watches and went home."

Tom would be more lenient, but only slightly: "I'd let the chronometers and computers go until twice the winning time has passed, then stop. Now we are up to 4:14 to 4:20 in elite marathons, and five hours in local marathons."

He claimed, "If a competitor can't finish in less than that time, officials rule the attempt as a nonfinish of the race. He or she is not a competitor and did not race the marathon. What you might call it is a 26.2-mile hike."

True, officials used to quit timing after four hours or so. This was because few runners finished slower. True, a runner who takes more than twice as long as the leader to finish isn't racing. "Surviving" is a better word.

But Tom's proposal is too radical. It would penalize the same people who are making the marathon grow into what it is today.

Tip for the Day

Pacers and Racers, use the walking breaks primarily as a training option. You can aim to eliminate the breaks on raceday, when the excitement of the event probably should make walking unnecessary.

Day 25

Date _____

Plan _____

Training for the Day

Training Session

Type   Long ____   Fast ____   Easy ____   Other (specify) _____

Distance _____   **Time** _____

Pace _____   **Splits** _____ / _____ / _____ / _____ / _____

Effort   Max ____   Hard ____   Moderate ____   Mild ____   Rest ____

Warm-up _____   **Cool-down** _____

Cross-training (specify) _____

Training Conditions

Location _____   **Time of day** _____

People   Trained alone ____   Trained w/partner ____   Trained w/group ____

Terrain _____   **Surface** _____

Temperature ____   **Humidity** ____   **Wind** ____   **Precipitation** _____

Training Grade for the Day

Physical status   A   B   C   D   F

Psychological status   A   B   C   D   F

Comments _____

_____

_____

Day 26

Thought for the Day

The Clock Runs On

We can't turn back the clock. The marathon will never again be the race it was when timing stopped at four hours. And for that we can rejoice.

Tom Derderian has spent his life watching, running, and writing about the Boston Marathon. This focus might have blurred his vision of the event as a whole.

Boston isn't typical. It isn't a workable model for marathons nationwide. Boston's qualifying times limit it to faster marathoners and allow the watches to stop early. Boston thrives despite these limits, not because of them.

But other marathons can't operate this way. They can't afford to set qualifying times for starters, or strict cutoff times for finishers. Marathons are growing and slowing. The new boom is from the middle of the pack on back.

I was truly a midpacker in the mid-1970s, with an equal number of runners going faster and slower. Now I run an hour slower than before, but *still* finish in midpack. More than half of us will take more than four hours to finish. But most of us will get there if the officials give us enough time.

It isn't an act of kindness to let the clocks run a couple of hours longer than they do at Boston. It's an act of self-interest for the officials. Marathoners who take more than twice as long as the leaders to finish now pay most of an event's bills. Marathons now depend on the survival runners for their own survival.

Tip for the Day

Cruisers, you can plan to continue taking walking breaks during the marathon. If your only goal is to cover the distance, use any trick that will take you to the finish line—and this trick is one of the most useful.

Day 26

Date _____

Plan _____

Training for the Day

Training Session

Type   Long ____   Fast ____   Easy ____   Other (specify) _____

Distance _____   **Time** _____

Pace _____   **Splits** _____ / _____ / _____ / _____ / _____

Effort   Max ____   Hard ____   Moderate ____   Mild ____   Rest ____

Warm-up _____   **Cool-down** _____

Cross-training (specify) _____

Training Conditions

Location _____   **Time of day** _____

People   Trained alone ____   Trained w/partner ____   Trained w/group ____

Terrain _____   **Surface** _____

Temperature ____   **Humidity** ____   **Wind** ____   **Precipitation** _____

Training Grade for the Day

Physical status	A	B	C	D	F
Psychological status	A	B	C	D	F

Comments _____

_____

_____

Day 27

Thought for the Day

Today's Marathoners

Their purple T-shirts with spotted owl artwork identified who they were and what they'd just done. Ten of them had run the Avenue of the Giants Marathon that day, and were now refueling and celebrating at a restaurant in Myers Flat, California.

They didn't know a diner at another table, but his purple shirt told them they spoke the same language. A woman of about 60 went over and introduced herself as Millie. "We're all from Portland," said Millie. "We like to travel to scenic marathons together—Crater Lake, Victoria, and now Avenue." She asked about future possibilities.

Here they'd just finished one marathon and were already planning the next. The time-honored Frank Shorter rule—which states that "you can't think of running another until you forget how bad the last one felt"—didn't cover them. They felt fine because they hadn't hurried. Their marathon wasn't a race but a long, slow run-hike. They'd be ready to take another like it in a few weeks.

If you haven't run this distance for a while, or haven't drifted back through the ranks, you may not have noticed how much marathoning has changed. It isn't the sport it used to be.

It's really two sports now. One side races for fast times and high places, while the other runs—and walks—to finish. The first sport is shrinking. The second has never been bigger or healthier.

Tip for the Day

Don't think you'll sacrifice a lot of time with walking breaks. A 1-minute break each mile totals 26 minutes of walking. But you still cover distance while walking and probably net only about 10 minutes lost.

Day 27

Date _____

Plan _____

Training for the Day

Training Session

Type   Long ____   Fast ____   Easy ____   Other (specify) _____

Distance _____   **Time** _____

Pace _____   **Splits** _____ / _____ / _____ / _____ / _____

Effort   Max ____   Hard ____   Moderate ____   Mild ____   Rest ____

Warm-up _____   **Cool-down** _____

Cross-training (specify) _____

Training Conditions

Location _____   **Time of day** _____

People Trained alone ____   Trained w/partner ____   Trained w/group ____

Terrain _____   **Surface** _____

Temperature ____   **Humidity** ____   **Wind** ____   **Precipitation** _____

Training Grade for the Day

Physical status   A   B   C   D   F

Psychological status   A   B   C   D   F

Comments _____

_____

_____

Day 28

Thought for the Day

Slowing of the Sport

Twenty years ago, the Boston Marathon qualifying time was 3:30. It's higher for some age groups and lower for others now, but still averages about 3:30. Thirty percent of Boston's runners broke three hours in the early 1970s. By now, in a field 10 times larger, the count of sub-threes has dropped to 10 percent.

The spring's biggest marathon is Los Angeles, where entries are unlimited. Only two percent of its nearly twenty thousand finishers run sub-threes.

Many races used to stop their clocks and open their roads at four hours, because so few runners came later. Now as many people finish after four hours as before at most marathons.

The new marathoners represent today's majority. Their marathon isn't a race but a survival test. It also can be a graduation exercise from an organized training program, a guided group tour, a social event, a minivacation.

The growth prospects of marathoning clearly lie with the second group. The most successful events of the future will be those catering to the needs and interests of the new marathoner—and to reformed racers who stroll over to the other side.

It's OK now to run slowly. It's OK to take walking breaks or even to walk all the way. It's not OK to say that U.S. marathoning is poorer today because the front ranks have thinned. Our wealth has simply dropped back an hour or so.

Tip for the Day

If you opt to walk in the marathon, plan to do so for a couple of minutes at each of the drink stations—usually spaced two or three miles apart. This insures that you'll swallow the drinks instead of gagging on them.

Day 28

Date _____

Plan _____

Training for the Day

Training Session

Type   Long ____   Fast ____   Easy ____   Other (specify) _____

Distance _____   **Time** _____

Pace _____   **Splits** _____ / _____ / _____ / _____ / _____

Effort   Max ____   Hard ____   Moderate ____   Mild ____   Rest ____

Warm-up _____   **Cool-down** _____

Cross-training (specify) _____

Training Conditions

Location _____   **Time of day** _____

People   Trained alone ____   Trained w/partner ____   Trained w/group ____

Terrain _____   **Surface** _____

Temperature ____   **Humidity** ____   **Wind** ____   **Precipitation** _____

Training Grade for the Day

Physical status   A   B   C   D   F

Psychological status   A   B   C   D   F

Comments _____

_____

_____

"Victory is mine!" this runner says with his smile. He has just completed the Columbus Marathon.

WEEK FIVE:
Setting Pace

We've talked about "projected marathon pace." But how do you project what you'll run? Get out a calculator and multiply your most recent 10K time by 5.0 (for Cruisers), 4.8 (for Pacers), or 4.6 (for Racers). For instance, 50 minutes times 5.0 equals a potential marathon time of 4:10, or about 9-1/2 minutes per mile. Choose your program below, assign workouts to the next seven days' diary pages, and add details there for completed training.

Cruiser Program
Big day: semi-long run of seven to eight miles, or half the distance of last week's long one. Run this distance nonstop, with no walking breaks. Run slightly faster than your projected marathon pace.
Other training days: three or four easy runs of 30 to 45 minutes each, with walking breaks optional.
Rest days: two or three with no running, but possibly cross-training.

Pacer Program
Big day: long run of 16 to 18 miles, or about a 2-mile increase from your last one. Walking breaks optional. Run about one minute per mile slower than your projected marathon pace.
Other training days: four to five easy runs of 30 to 60 minutes each.
Rest days: one or two with no running, but possibly cross-training.

Racer Program
Long day: long run of 18 to 20 miles, or about a 2-mile increase from the last one. Run about one minute per mile slower than marathon pace.
Fast day: one- to three-mile run at current 10K race pace (this may be broken into shorter intervals that total one to three miles, not counting recovery periods). Warm up and cool down with easy running.
Other training days: four easy runs of 30 to 60 minutes each.
Rest days: one with no running, but possibly cross-training.

Day 29

Thought for the Day

What Price, PRs?

My son isn't following in his dad's footsteps. He is leading the old man. In just his second meet as a high school freshman, Eric beat the fastest sprint times I ever ran. Better yet, he already had caught onto the idea of personal records. Eric realizes he doesn't need to beat everyone, or *anyone*, to win his race. He can win by improving his time.

The trouble with times is that they don't always tell the truth. Especially in high school track, where volunteers who've never before held a watch do much of the timing.

Eric's "official" time in a 100-meter race his first season read a half-second faster than the one on my watch—and faster by an equal amount than his PR. He wanted very much to believe the rookie timer.

I told him that the false time would come back to haunt him in later races. He would run slower and might think he had failed, even while breaking his true PR. A 16-year-old never admits that his dad is right. But the next week, Eric boasted of "tying my best time"—the true one.

Inflated times don't lay traps just for kids. Runners of all ages and at all distances want desperately to believe the best news a watch can offer. Long ago, before digital wristwatches and certified courses arrived, I set many PRs that were too good to be true. Accepting the truth wasn't easy. But accepting the false times would have erected an artificial barrier to my progress.

Tip for the Day

Simulate the marathon distance in long runs, but at a slower pace. Mimic racing pace in your fast runs, but only at a shorter distance. Combine full distance at full pace only when it counts: in the race itself.

Day 29

Date _____

Plan _____

Training for the Day

Training Session

Type   Long ____   Fast ____   Easy ____   Other (specify) _____

Distance _____   **Time** _____

Pace _____   **Splits** _____ / _____ / _____ / _____ / _____

Effort   Max ____   Hard ____   Moderate ____   Mild ____   Rest ____

Warm-up _____   **Cool-down** _____

Cross-training (specify) _____

Training Conditions

Location _____   **Time of day** _____

People   Trained alone ____   Trained w/partner ____   Trained w/group ____

Terrain _____   **Surface** _____

Temperature ____   **Humidity** ____   **Wind** ____   **Precipitation** _____

Training Grade for the Day

Physical status   A   B   C   D   F

Psychological status   A   B   C   D   F

Comments _____

_____

_____

Day 30

Thought for the Day

Time of Your Life

I once improved by four seconds in a half-mile time trial—only later admitting that I'd carried a stopwatch that surely had lost time along the way. I once improved my 10K time by three minutes—only later accepting that the course must have been short by at least that amount.

Watches work better now, and courses are more accurate. Today's personal-record inflation often comes from slope and wind.

The 1994 Boston Marathon had both, and the times reflected the double benefit. The course descends by more than three meters per kilometer, compared with a limit of one meter for national records. Boston officials refuted reports of 19-mile-an-hour tailwinds, but readings averaged a helpful 7 miles per hour. Nowhere have so many men and women run so fast.

How these times appear on record lists doesn't concern me as much as how these PRs might affect the runners. Everyone who ran fast in Boston now wants to think this new level is the true one.

Women's winner Uta Pippig improved by 4-1/2 minutes. Cosmas Ndeti ran more than 2 minutes faster than ever before while winning the men's race.

What happens the next time they and countless other Boston PR setters run under neutral conditions? They'll probably run their normal times and wonder, "What went wrong?"

If you choose to believe that times from aided courses like these are true PRs, prepare to live in their shadow.

Tip for the Day

Complement your long runs with some that are semi-long. These let you know how it feels to run at marathon pace for an extended distance, while still not overwhelming you with their length and degree of difficulty.

Day 30

Date _____

Plan _____

Training for the Day

Training Session

Type   Long ____   Fast ____   Easy ____   Other (specify) _____

Distance _____   **Time** _____

Pace _____   **Splits** _____ / _____ / _____ / _____ / _____

Effort   Max ____   Hard ____   Moderate ____   Mild ____   Rest ____

Warm-up _____   **Cool-down** _____

Cross-training (specify) _____

Training Conditions

Location _____   **Time of day** _____

People   Trained alone ____   Trained w/partner ____   Trained w/group ____

Terrain _____   **Surface** _____

Temperature ____   **Humidity** ____   **Wind** ____   **Precipitation** _____

Training Grade for the Day

Physical status   A   B   C   D   F

Psychological status   A   B   C   D   F

Comments _____

_____

_____

Day 31

Thought for the Day

PRs That Aren't

Marathoners don't descend on St. George, Utah, in record numbers each fall to admire its red-rock canyons. They don't drop in on the California International to enjoy the December weather. They go there for the courses. *Runner's World* listed these two marathons among America's fastest, and they are among the places to qualify for the Olympic Trials and the Boston Marathon.

U.S. records can't count as "unaided" if the course slopes more than one meter per kilometer. But neither Boston nor the Trials puts any gradient limit on qualifying races.

St. George goes downhill at a rate of 9 meters per kilometer, and Cal International at 2-1/2 meters. Times there earn tickets to the big races. I have no complaint with that. The Men's and Women's Trials aren't crowded, and the Boston course itself goes downhill (at 3-1/2 times the record limit). I don't begrudge anyone the chance to run one of those races.

But maybe we should rename these aided times as "P-Aren'ts." As one whose fastest marathon came on an aided course, I say that you count such a time at your peril. The downhill mark will come back to haunt you, as mine did me until I realized its true meaning.

My Boston P-Aren't was a novelty item. Like a wind-boosted sprint time or a short-course road time, it didn't compare with valid marks. By accepting downhill times as PRs, you lay a trap for yourself. The only way to break these "records" is to seek courses that are *more* aided. Two meters per kilometer of assistance becomes 10 meters, then . . . What next, free-falling off a cliff?

Tip for the Day

Between long runs, take some that are about half the distance of the latest long session. If you've just run 20 miles, for instance, do 10 this time—but at your projected marathon pace or slightly faster.

Day 31

Date _____

Plan _____

Training for the Day

Training Session

Type   Long ____   Fast ____   Easy ____   Other (specify) _____

Distance _____   **Time** _____

Pace _____   **Splits** _____ / _____ / _____ / _____ / _____

Effort   Max ____   Hard ____   Moderate ____   Mild ____   Rest ____

Warm-up _____   **Cool-down** _____

Cross-training (specify) _____

Training Conditions

Location _____   **Time of day** _____

People   Trained alone ____   Trained w/partner ____   Trained w/group ____

Terrain _____   **Surface** _____

Temperature ____   **Humidity** ____   **Wind** ____   **Precipitation** _____

Training Grade for the Day

Physical status   A   B   C   D   F

Psychological status   A   B   C   D   F

Comments _____

_____

_____

Day 32

Thought for the Day

Fairly Fast Marathons

You've read my spiels the last few days about setting inflated PRs on courses with slope and wind assistance. The next logical question is "What are the fastest *unaided* marathon courses?"

Most of the memorable American times have been run downhill, with help from the wind, or both. Courses that USATF record keepers call aided account for the eight fastest men's marathons and five of the top eight women's times. Most of those were run at Boston.

Others receiving too much help from gravity: California International at Sacramento, Grandma's, St. George, and Las Vegas. Still others are flat enough but can catch favorable breezes because of their point-to-point design. New York City falls into this gray zone of maybe aided, maybe not.

Fifty U.S. men have run 2:12 or better, and an equal number of women have gone 2:35 or faster. Of these 100 runners, 38 ran their times on just three aided courses—Boston, Cal International, and Grandma's.

So what are the best times by Americans on fully legal U.S. courses? The women's answer is easy. The fastest and most legit are the same—Joan Samuelson's 2:21:21 at Chicago in 1985. For men, Jerry Lawson's 2:09:35 at Chicago 1997 ranks ninth on the all-time, all-conditions list.

The list of elite 100 American marathoners also favors Twin Cities. The Minnesota race contributes 11 marks to lead all events that get no excessive aid from slope or wind.

Tip for the Day

As with the long runs, make each semi-long one a marathon rehearsal. Run a similar course at the same time of day, and dress and drink as you would on the actual marathon day.

Day 32

Date _____

Plan _____

Training for the Day

Training Session

Type   Long ____   Fast ____   Easy ____   Other (specify) ____

Distance _____   **Time** _____

Pace _____   **Splits** _____ / _____ / _____ / _____ / _____

Effort   Max ____   Hard ____   Moderate ____   Mild ____   Rest ____

Warm-up _____   **Cool-down** _____

Cross-training (specify) _____

Training Conditions

Location _____   **Time of day** _____

People   Trained alone ____   Trained w/partner ____   Trained w/group ____

Terrain _____   **Surface** _____

Temperature ____   **Humidity** ____   **Wind** ____   **Precipitation** _____

Training Grade for the Day

Physical status   A   B   C   D   F

Psychological status   A   B   C   D   F

Comments _____

_____

_____

Day 33

Thought for the Day

Neutral Sites

The five marathons with the best histories of fast times on fair (unaided by slope or wind) routes are Twin Cities, Houston-Tenneco, Chicago, Pittsburgh, and Los Angeles. However, the nature of some of these events skews the figures somewhat.

Unlike many marathons its size, Twin Cities emphasizes American fields that tend to produce faster times here than elsewhere. Houston and Pittsburgh hosted Olympic Trials for women, and those two races supplied most of the best times.

My nominees to round out the current top 10, where the amenities of a good-sized race combine with chances to set true PRs:

- Cleveland Revco, where men have run sub-2:12 and women in the low 2:30s

- Columbus, where all three male Olympians ran in the 2:12s to make the 1992 team

- Disney World, where numbers, flat course, and winter date are sure to produce great times in coming years

- Long Beach, where men have run about 2:13 and women around 2:35

- Portland, where many records were set in the old Cascade Run Off on similar terrain

One of the fastest loop courses has gone unused since the Nike-OTC Marathon retired in the mid-1980s. Joan Benoit set an American record of 2:26:11 and four men broke 2:11 on the Eugene course.

Tip for the Day

If you enter races longer than 10 kilometers, treat them strictly as semi-long training runs instead of competitions. If the event is a half-marathon, run it at *marathon* pace and not all out.

Day 33

Date _____

Plan _____

Training for the Day

Training Session

Type   Long ____   Fast ____   Easy ____   Other (specify) _____

Distance _____   **Time** _____

Pace _____   **Splits** _____ / _____ / _____ / _____ / _____

Effort   Max ____   Hard ____   Moderate ____   Mild ____   Rest ____

Warm-up _____   **Cool-down** _____

Cross-training (specify) _____

Training Conditions

Location _____   **Time of day** _____

People   Trained alone ____   Trained w/partner ____   Trained w/group ____

Terrain _____   **Surface** _____

Temperature ____   **Humidity** ____   **Wind** ____   **Precipitation** _____

Training Grade for the Day

Physical status   A   B   C   D   F

Psychological status   A   B   C   D   F

Comments _____

_____

_____

Day 34

Thought for the Day

The American Way

A reader of my magazine column asked what I thought of Colman McCarthy's piece in the *Washington Post*, titled "American Marathoners Running on Empty."

Not much. Oh, McCarthy is a fine writer. His prose flows so smoothly that his arguments sound convincing—if you don't look too closely at the facts. McCarthy points out, rightly, that no American would come within miles of the 1995 New York City Marathon winner. None did. The first U.S. man trailed by 11 minutes, the top native woman by more than 20.

The *Post* writer then asks, "How have U.S. runners become so run-of-the-mill?" Then he answers his own question. "Start with the obvious. The American diet of sugary, salty, and gunk-and-junk foods might as well be a weighted saddle bag. Fast foods don't fuel fast times. . . . World-class Kenyan marathoners train on world-class foods."

McCarthy's "second reason U.S. marathoners can't keep pace with Latin Americans and Africans is the American belief that we are all but constitutionally guaranteed pain-free living. Marathons hurt. No pill yet has been marketed to get people through, around, over or under The Wall." He concludes that "the era of Bill Rodgers, who won four New Yorks and three Bostons from 1976 to 1980, is gone."

Maybe no one from the United States will ever win as much as Rodgers did in the 1970s. But recall that Alberto Salazar and Joan Samuelson were almost as dominant in the 1980s, and that as recently as 1994 Bob Kempainen ran faster than any American—ever.

Tip for the Day

Practice running at or near marathon pace in some or all of your easy runs. This won't seem very fast or hard when you're averaging less than one-quarter the marathon distance on easy days.

Day 34

Date _____

Plan _____

Training for the Day

Training Session

Type   Long ____   Fast ____   Easy ____   Other (specify) _____

Distance _____   **Time** _____

Pace _____   **Splits** _____ / _____ / _____ / _____ / _____

Effort   Max ____   Hard ____   Moderate ____   Mild ____   Rest ____

Warm-up _____   **Cool-down** _____

Cross-training (specify) _____

Training Conditions

Location _____   **Time of day** _____

People   Trained alone ____   Trained w/partner ____   Trained w/group ____

Terrain _____   **Surface** _____

Temperature ____   **Humidity** ____   **Wind** ____   **Precipitation** _____

Training Grade for the Day

Physical status	A	B	C	D	F
Psychological status	A	B	C	D	F

Comments _____

_____

_____

Day 35

Thought for the Day

Americans at Their Best

Washington Post columnist Colman McCarthy penned an indictment of the state of the sport in this country. The title summarized his position: "American Marathoners Running on Empty."

McCarthy placed much of the blame on slovenly eating and training habits. American marathoners of all abilities should take offense with this blanket indictment of us as work-avoiding junk swillers. I've sat down to eat with hundreds of U.S. runners. As a group, they watch their diets closely—certainly eating much better than Bill Rodgers and most other marathoners did 20 years ago.

McCarthy says Americans seek ease. Then explain why, by a more important standard than international victories and record times, this country is unchallenged as the world leader. The United States has far more marathoners per capita than any other country. More than three times as many runners from here go this distance now than ran it 20 years ago.

So what happened to the top Americans at New York City 1995, which the *Post* columnist used as his example of the decline in national talent? The best runners weren't there because they were training for the Olympic Trials three months later, as they should have been. Even NYC Marathon director Allan Steinfeld said, "That [opportunity to compete in the Trials] is not something you turn down. Running for your country is the best that you can do."

A smart runner knows not to run too many marathons and knows how to wait for the ones that count the most. By that standard, Americans are smarter—if not faster—than they used to be.

Tip for the Day

Don't bother measuring each course precisely and timing every mile of it. Just take occasional spot checks for known distances (such as a few laps of a track) to monitor your pace.

Day 35

Date _____

Plan _____

Training for the Day

Training Session

Type　　Long ____　Fast ____　Easy ____　Other (specify) _____

Distance _____　**Time** _____

Pace _____　**Splits** _____ / _____ / _____ / _____ / _____

Effort　　Max ____　Hard ____　Moderate ____　Mild ____　Rest ____

Warm-up _____　**Cool-down** _____

Cross-training (specify) _____

Training Conditions

Location _____　**Time of day** _____

People　Trained alone ____　Trained w/partner ____　Trained w/group ____

Terrain _____　**Surface** _____

Temperature ____　**Humidity** ____　**Wind** ____　**Precipitation** _____

Training Grade for the Day

Physical status	A	B	C	D	F
Psychological status	A	B	C	D	F

Comments _____

_____

_____

Note the feet of these marathoners in Berlin. Many are walking, which has become an accepted part of the event.

WEEK SIX:
Learning Tricks

This week's Tips theme is upping your tempo. Semi-long runs, fast runs, and short races all serve the same purpose. They acquaint you with the pace or tempo of your marathon, and often ask you to run somewhat faster. While learning these tricks, check the Thoughts for additional shared wisdom on the sport. Choose your program below, assign workouts to the next seven days' diary pages, and add details there for completed training.

Cruiser Program
Big day: race of five kilometers, or fast solo run of one to three miles. In either case, run at least one minute per mile faster than your projected marathon pace.
Other training days: three or four easy runs of 30 to 45 minutes each, with walking breaks optional.
Rest days: two or three with no running, but possibly cross-training.

Pacer Program
Big day: semi-long run of eight to nine miles, or half the distance of last week's long one. Run this distance nonstop, at your projected marathon pace or slightly faster.
Other training days: four to five easy runs of 30 to 60 minutes each.
Rest days: one or two with no running, but possibly cross-training.

Racer Program
Long day: semi-long run of 9 to 10 miles, or half the distance of last week's long one. Run at your projected marathon pace or slightly faster.
Fast day: race of 5K to 10K, or one- to three-mile run at current 10K race pace (this may be broken into shorter intervals that total one to three miles, not counting recovery periods). Warm up and cool down with easy running.
Other training days: four easy runs of 30 to 60 minutes each.
Rest days: one with no running, but possibly cross-training.

Day 36

Thought for the Day

Knowing and Showing

We had met the day before, and I'd taken an instant liking to him. At any other time, we might have talked running techniques for hours. But early in a marathon wasn't the time. He was a skilled ultrarunner, I a mere marathoner, and he wanted to share his hard-won wisdom on eating, drinking, footwear, hill climbing, and pacing.

He meant well, but I didn't want his advice just then. I excused myself from his company at five miles to take care of the remaining business my way.

A little later, I passed two experienced-looking men. One said, "Slow down, you have a long way to go." Then when he thought I was beyond earshot, he told his partner, "He'll break down." I shouted back over my shoulder, "Wanna bet?" The two men soon saw me taking a (planned) walk, and they traded I-told-you-so looks.

The irony is that I wanted to do just what these advisers had done. I saw runners going wrong and wanted to set them right. Only some tongue biting kept me from giving unsolicited advice. This wasn't the time.

You might think that today's runners all know the rules. They have books and magazines to read, and veterans nearby who'd be happy to help. But the makeup of races—especially marathons— is changing. The number of newcomers—especially young ones— is climbing again. Many of them haven't yet plugged into the advice channels.

You might already know what to do. But you can help novices by passing along tips when the time is right—*before* their next race.

Tip for the Day

Build faster running into your program for several reasons: It lifts you out of a one-pace rut, adds variety to training, and gives you something challenging to do on weekends between long runs.

Day 36

Date _____

Plan _____

Training for the Day

Training Session

Type Long ____ Fast ____ Easy ____ Other (specify) _____

Distance _____ **Time** _____

Pace _____ **Splits** _____ / _____ / _____ / _____ / _____

Effort Max ____ Hard ____ Moderate ____ Mild ____ Rest ____

Warm-up _____ **Cool-down** _____

Cross-training (specify) _____

Training Conditions

Location _____ **Time of day** _____

People Trained alone ____ Trained w/partner ____ Trained w/group ____

Terrain _____ **Surface** _____

Temperature ____ **Humidity** ____ **Wind** ____ **Precipitation** _____

Training Grade for the Day

Physical status   A   B   C   D   F

Psychological status   A   B   C   D   F

Comments _____

_____

_____

Day 37

Thought for the Day

Miles of Trials

Oldtimers' tricks that I would like to have passed along to newer runners during one marathon—Napa Valley:

- Dress down. Napa's cloudy, calm, cool day was perfect for a marathon. It was shorts-and-singlet weather. Yet I saw tights and long-sleeved shirts, even jackets and gloves. These runners hadn't yet learned that clothing feeling comfortable at the starting line will quickly become too warm.

- Test shoes. At Napa, many runners wore shoes that appeared to be fresh out of the box, and some acquired bloodstains as the miles piled up. No one had told their wearers to use no shoe in the marathon that hadn't passed the tests of training.

- Start cold. I watched new runners jog the mile from their parked cars to the start, while the vets walked slowly—and would have hitched rides if possible. Know that warm-up runs waste valuable steps and lead to starting too fast.

- Drink early. I heard runners say while bypassing the first station, two miles along, "I'm not thirsty yet." Of course not, but that's what runners must learn: Drink to delay dehydration later on, not to satisfy thirst now.

- Cut corners. Napa's course featured many sweeping curves in the early miles. The road was closed to traffic, but I saw runners staying in their lane around each bend. They should know that cutting corners is legal and a straight line is still the shortest distance between two points.

Tip for the Day

Find a cure for "one-pace syndrome." It afflicts runners who know how to run long but have never learned to run fast. They run the same pace in races as in training, in 5Ks as in marathons.

Day 37

Date _____

Plan _____

Training for the Day

Training Session

Type Long _____ Fast _____ Easy _____ Other (specify) _____

Distance _____ **Time** _____

Pace _____ **Splits** _____ / _____ / _____ / _____ / _____

Effort Max _____ Hard _____ Moderate _____ Mild _____ Rest _____

Warm-up _____ **Cool-down** _____

Cross-training (specify) _____

Training Conditions

Location _____ **Time of day** _____

People Trained alone _____ Trained w/partner _____ Trained w/group _____

Terrain _____ **Surface** _____

Temperature _____ **Humidity** _____ **Wind** _____ **Precipitation** _____

Training Grade for the Day

Physical status   A   B   C   D   F

Psychological status   A   B   C   D   F

Comments _____

_____

_____

Day 38

Thought for the Day

Ain't It the Truth?

A few truisms of the sport, gathered from almost 40 years of running and recording the thoughts of runners:

- The hardest step in any run is the first one out the door.
- You never know how a run will go until you've gone at least a mile.
- The real running begins after a half-hour warm-up, and the run starts to seem like a second job after an hour.
- Training courses are usually shorter than you want to believe.
- Runners round times down and round distances up.
- Time doesn't pass at a constant rate; the harder the run, the longer a minute seems to last.
- You never make up running downhill what you lose going uphill; same with tailwinds and headwinds.
- Even if you believe in walking breaks, you're embarrassed to be seen taking them.
- You can't run past a store window without sneaking a peek at yourself.
- A "jogger" is someone who runs slower than you do.
- Fitness is a stage you pass through on the way to becoming a "real runner" who no longer settles for merely staying fit.
- Drivers don't see road runners smile because we're too busy concentrating on not getting run over.
- Sports drinks and energy bars only taste good when you need them most.

Tip for the Day

Avoid training for maximum speed right now. But also don't let it be a time for neglecting speed entirely, which can easily happen when you're piling up all those slow miles.

Day 38

Date _____

Plan _____

Training for the Day

Training Session

Type   Long _____   Fast _____   Easy _____   Other (specify) _____

Distance _____   **Time** _____

Pace _____   **Splits** _____ / _____ / _____ / _____ / _____

Effort   Max _____   Hard _____   Moderate _____   Mild _____   Rest _____

Warm-up _____   **Cool-down** _____

Cross-training (specify) _____

Training Conditions

Location _____   **Time of day** _____

People   Trained alone _____   Trained w/partner _____   Trained w/group _____

Terrain _____   **Surface** _____

Temperature _____   **Humidity** _____   **Wind** _____   **Precipitation** _____

Training Grade for the Day

Physical status   A   B   C   D   F

Psychological status   A   B   C   D   F

Comments _____ _____

_____

_____

Day 39

Thought for the Day

Better Believe It

More truisms of the sport:

- If you feel warm enough at the start of a run, you're overdressed and will soon overheat.
- Most running injuries aren't accidental but are self-inflicted.
- Most injuries will respond to the treatment you least want to use: stopping the running that caused them.
- Racing a long distance on a hard surface at a fast pace is an unnatural act, which never stopped anyone from doing it.
- If you aren't scared before a race, worry that you aren't ready.
- No matter how fast you run your race, someone, somewhere will always be faster.
- No matter how slow you go in this race, someone will be slower; you can't finish last no matter how hard you try.
- "Official" times are rarely accurate, which is why you start your watch when *you* cross the starting line.
- Races don't feel worst at the end, but in the middle third where the start and finish both seem so far away.
- It's more fun to pass than to be passed late in a race, which is another reason to start slowly.
- Your fastest races feel the easiest, because you trained for and paced them best.
- If you'd known when you were younger what you know now, you would have made different mistakes.

Tip for the Day

Benefit from a few fast runs. Faster training makes you a faster runner at all distances, including the marathon. A 10-second improvement per mile translates to almost *4-1/2 minutes* for a marathoner.

Day 39

Date _____

Plan _____

Training for the Day

Training Session

Type   Long ____   Fast ____   Easy ____   Other (specify) _____

Distance _____   **Time** _____

Pace _____   **Splits** _____ / _____ / _____ / _____ / _____

Effort   Max ____   Hard ____   Moderate ____   Mild ____   Rest ____

Warm-up _____   **Cool-down** _____

Cross-training (specify) _____

Training Conditions

Location _____   **Time of day** _____

People Trained alone ____   Trained w/partner ____   Trained w/group ____

Terrain _____   **Surface** _____

Temperature ____   **Humidity** ____   **Wind** ____   **Precipitation** _____

Training Grade for the Day

Physical status   A   B   C   D   F

Psychological status   A   B   C   D   F

Comments _____

_____

_____

Day 40

Thought for the Day

Rules We Run By

Rick Reilly, the resident humorist at *Sports Illustrated*, wrote down some previously unwritten rules of sports in a column. He included one about our sport: "Always clear the inside lane for faster runners." I'd never seen that edict spelled out before. But somehow I always knew that the common law of running awarded the pole position to the person doing the passing.

Etiquette, tradition, and superstition dictate many of our moves. Written or not, these are rules we run by. For instance:

- Never use the J-word to describe your activity. Always think of yourself as a "serious runner," no matter how much fun you have.

- Never wear a T-shirt from a race you haven't finished. Always wear your marathon shirts on occasions when impressions count most.

- Never ask a runner at work to stop and talk. Always wave at the runners you meet, even if you've never seen them before.

- Never quote your true weekly mileage. Instead give a figure for an ideal week. Always add, "But these are *quality* miles."

- Never buy running shoes from anyone who calls them sneakers. Always keep searching for the perfect shoe, whatever the cost.

- Never trust a weatherperson who says, "It's a perfect day." Always take that to mean perfect for the beach, bad for a run.

- Never trust drivers to slow, stop, or signal for a runner.

Tip for the Day

Check this bonus: Added speed translates to faster racing with no apparent increase in effort. And an occasional speedy run makes marathon pace seem easier than if you'd trained only at the slower rate.

Day 40

Date _____

Plan _____

Training for the Day

Training Session

Type   Long ____   Fast ____   Easy ____   Other (specify) _____

Distance _____   **Time** _____

Pace _____   **Splits** _____ / _____ / _____ / _____ / _____

Effort   Max ____   Hard ____   Moderate ____   Mild ____   Rest ____

Warm-up _____   **Cool-down** _____

Cross-training (specify) _____

Training Conditions

Location _____   **Time of day** _____

People   Trained alone ____   Trained w/partner ____   Trained w/group ____

Terrain _____   **Surface** _____

Temperature ____   **Humidity** ____   **Wind** ____   **Precipitation** _____

Training Grade for the Day

Physical status   A   B   C   D   F

Psychological status   A   B   C   D   F

Comments _____

_____

_____

Day 41

Thought for the Day

Running's Rules

More rules to run by:

- Never trust a doctor who says, "If it hurts to run, then stop running." Always find one who'll let you keep hurting yourself.

- Never trust a race director who calls a course "flat and fast." Always prepare for a long, hard day when you read "gently rolling hills."

- Never admit that you feel healthy and fit before a race. Always sound like you're newly released from intensive care.

- Never line up on the front row at a race unless you run five-minute miles or want five-minute milers running up your back. Always line up ahead of your expected-pace sign unless you like to run over slower people.

- Never start your watch when the gun fires but when you cross the starting line. Always round your final time down, as in calling it 39 minutes for anything under 39:59.

- Never spit into the wind. Always look beside you before blowing your nose in a crowd.

- Never say, "I'll never let a woman (or a heavyweight, or a kid) beat me," because one always will. Always let kamikaze kickers pass you in the final yards.

- Never shove ahead of another runner in the chute. Always say, "Good race," to the runner ahead of and the runner behind you at the end.

Tip for the Day

In your speedwork, try to average at least one minute per mile faster than your long-run and easy-day pace. If the slower running averages eight minutes per mile, for instance, speed up to seven minutes or faster.

Day 41

Date _____

Plan _____

Training for the Day

Training Session

Type   Long ____   Fast ____   Easy ____   Other (specify) _____

Distance _____   **Time** _____

Pace _____ **Splits** _____ / _____ / _____ / _____ / _____

Effort   Max ____   Hard ____   Moderate ____   Mild ____   Rest ____

Warm-up _____   **Cool-down** _____

Cross-training (specify) _____

Training Conditions

Location _____   **Time of day** _____

People   Trained alone ____   Trained w/partner ____   Trained w/group ____

Terrain _____   **Surface** _____

Temperature ____   **Humidity** ____   **Wind** ____   **Precipitation** _____

Training Grade for the Day

Physical status   A   B   C   D   F

Psychological status   A   B   C   D   F

Comments _____

_____

_____

Day 42

Thought for the Day

Mah's Ways

"Sy Mah spent his last 20 years breaking the rules," I said at the program on ultraendurance sports, held in honor of the late University of Toledo professor. "He was an exercise scientist who didn't follow the rules of exercise science."

Mah ran more marathons than anyone else had at the time—524 in all. But he didn't train for them, taper for them, or recover from them in the approved ways. Sy averaged one marathon every other week for almost 20 years, often doubled on a weekend, sometimes tripled on a three-day weekend, and once ran five marathons in nine days. Yet he wasn't so much breaking rules as *making* those that worked for him.

The standard rules fit the typical marathoner: one who runs nearly every day and often hard, and who runs marathons—along with all other races—as fast as possible. Sy Mah wasn't typical.

His first rule was to *run* marathons, not race them. He usually ran at least a minute per mile slower than his best possible pace, and he often stopped to walk with runners who were having trouble.

Mah's second rule was to train little during the week and to save his big efforts for the weekends. "He didn't care much for any kind of training," says his friend Willie Williamson. "I doubt if he ran more than 20 miles a week between races, and his runs were very rarely longer than 5 or 6 miles."

Mah's marathons *were* his training. He lived for his marathon weekends. On a videotape that Williamson saved, Sy says, "My weekends were very full and tremendously exciting."

Tip for the Day

Save your really fast running for later—after the marathon ends and recovery from it is complete. The strength you gain now will lay the groundwork for faster racing when your emphasis shifts to speed.

Day 42

Date _____

Plan _____

Training for the Day

Training Session

Type   Long ____   Fast ____   Easy ____   Other (specify) _____

Distance _____   **Time** _____

Pace _____   **Splits** _____ / _____ / _____ / _____ / _____

Effort   Max ____   Hard ____   Moderate ____   Mild ____   Rest ____

Warm-up _____   **Cool-down** _____

Cross-training (specify) _____

Training Conditions

Location _____   **Time of day** _____

People   Trained alone ____   Trained w/partner ____   Trained w/group ____

Terrain _____   **Surface** _____

Temperature ____   **Humidity** ____   **Wind** ____   **Precipitation** _____

Training Grade for the Day

Physical status   A   B   C   D   F

Psychological status   A   B   C   D   F

Comments _____

_____

_____

The most spectacular start in marathoning: Runners stream across the
Verrazano Narrows Bridge in New York City.

WEEK SEVEN:
Picking Races

You pass the midpoint in the training program this week. Look how far you've come—to within 5 to 10 miles of the marathon distance. The long run for Cruisers averages 17 miles, for Pacers 19 miles, and for Racers 21 miles. The race is becoming real to you, so we'll talk in this week's Thoughts about the menu of available marathons and in the Tips about shorter races. Choose your program below, assign workouts to the next seven days' diary pages, and add details there for completed training.

Cruiser Program
Big day: long run of 16 to 18 miles, or about a 2-mile increase from your last one. Mix running and walking while covering the distance no faster than your projected marathon pace.
Other training days: three or four easy runs of 30 to 45 minutes each, with walking breaks optional.
Rest days: two or three with no running, but possibly cross-training.

Pacer Program
Big day: long run of 18 to 20 miles, or about a 2-mile increase from your last one. Walking breaks optional. Run about one minute per mile slower than your projected marathon pace.
Other training days: four to five easy runs of 30 to 60 minutes each.
Rest days: one or two with no running, but possibly cross-training.

Racer Program
Long day: long run of 20 to 22 miles, or about a 2-mile increase from your last one. Run about one minute per mile slower than marathon pace.
Fast day: one- to three-mile run at current 10K race pace (this may be broken into shorter intervals that total one to three miles, not counting recovery periods). Warm up and cool down with easy running.
Other training days: four easy runs of 30 to 60 minutes each.
Rest days: one with no running, but possibly cross-training.

Day 43

Thought for the Day

Boston's Biographer

You know you're aging when you knew the esteemed historian of the world's most historic race while he was still a kid. Tom Derderian floated west from Massachusetts on a college break in 1970 and camped out on the floor of my cow barn-turned-apartment.

He was 20 then. A quarter century later, he published the deliciously detailed 600-page book *Boston Marathon: The History of the World's Premier Running Event.*

"My intention in writing," said Derderian in a letter that came with my copy, "was that the sheer mass of the book, devoid of nerdish statistics and paeans to the courage of the common runner, would empower our sport by memorializing its uncommon contenders. I wanted a book free of proselytizing but full of reverence and curiosity. I didn't want a how-to book but a how-it-was book."

He more than succeeded. This is more than a Boston history, more than a history of marathons generally. It's the history of distance running in the United States. All the historic names are here, because for most of the past 100 years all roads eventually led to Boston.

Derderian likened his work on the book to running a marathon. (A multiyear streak of 100-mile training weeks might be a better analogy.) "But now that it is done," he wrote, "I bask in the euphoria of completion." You'll say the same after you've worked through these 600 pages. You'll thank Tom Derderian for this gratifying trip through history.

Tip for the Day

Plan to enter some 5K, 8K, or 10K races on weekends between long runs. The best place to build speed is in these short races. But don't take them so seriously that they detract from the marathon training.

Day 43

Date _____

Plan _____

Training for the Day

Training Session

Type   Long ____   Fast ____   Easy ____   Other (specify) _____

Distance _____   **Time** _____

Pace _____   **Splits** _____ / _____ / _____ / _____ / _____

Effort   Max ____   Hard ____   Moderate ____   Mild ____   Rest ____

Warm-up _____   **Cool-down** _____

Cross-training (specify) _____

Training Conditions

Location _____   **Time of day** _____

People   Trained alone ____   Trained w/partner ____   Trained w/group ____

Terrain _____   **Surface** _____

Temperature ____   **Humidity** ____   **Wind** ____   **Precipitation** _____

Training Grade for the Day

Physical status	A	B	C	D	F
Psychological status	A	B	C	D	F

Comments _____

_____

_____

Day 44

Thought for the Day

Historic Footnotes

Much as we'd like to take the credit, our generation didn't invent running as we know it. The roots of the modern sport were sunk long before we came along. Tom Derderian's *Boston Marathon* book reveals fact after surprising fact from the years before running boomed:

- 1844. Professional races existed 150 years ago, with a 10-mile race paying its winner $1,400.

- 1899. Manufacturers advertised shoes for marathon runners at $2 a pair.

- 1901. The Boston leaders, showing more speed than sense, ran the first (downhill) mile in 4:40 at a time when the American record for a single mile was only 4:15.

- 1905. The Rosie Ruiz of his era, Fred Lorz, redeemed himself by winning Boston after admitting to hitching a ride at the St. Louis Olympics the year before.

- 1906. Timmy Ford showed that marathoning wasn't just a grownup's game as he won Boston at 18.

- 1907. Boston winner Tom Longboat employed hard-easy training. Derderian writes, "Longboat allowed himself a full recovery from hard efforts so his body had time to strengthen itself before the next onslaught."

- 1910. Peter Foley might have been the first master. When Foley entered that year's race at age 52, officials barred him because "he was too old and had no chance to win." He ran anyway and continued to appear in the results until age 61.

Tip for the Day

Limit your races to 10K during the marathon-training period. That way, you'll get the full speed benefit from them and still not need more than a few days to recover from the short races.

Day 44

Date _____

Plan _____

Training for the Day

Training Session

Type　　Long ____　Fast ____　Easy ____　Other (specify) _____

Distance _____　**Time** _____

Pace _____ **Splits** _____ / _____ / _____ / _____ / _____

Effort　　Max ____　Hard ____　Moderate ____　Mild ____　Rest ____

Warm-up _____　**Cool-down** _____

Cross-training (specify) _____

Training Conditions

Location _____　**Time of day** _____

People　Trained alone ____　Trained w/partner ____　Trained w/group ____

Terrain _____　**Surface** _____

Temperature ____　**Humidity** ____　**Wind** ____　**Precipitation** _____

Training Grade for the Day

Physical status　　　　　A　　　B　　　C　　　D　　　F

Psychological status　　A　　　B　　　C　　　D　　　F

Comments _____

_____

_____

Day 45

Thought for the Day

Marathon Milestones

Continuing the quick trip through Boston Marathon history, with author Tom Derderian as our guide:

- 1911. Derderian tells of the first running boom. "Hundreds of marathon races were scheduled in the United States that year. In Massachusetts alone, there were Patriots' Day running races in nearly every town."

- 1924. Ads for $10 running shoes appeared, featuring endorser Clarence DeMar as the Michael Jordan of his day.

- 1935. Several top runners, including winner Johnny Kelley, wore custom-made white racing shoes at Boston. They weighed only 5-1/2 ounces per shoe.

- 1937. DeMar used a form of carbo loading that he called an elimination diet. It consisted of "a week of eating only fresh, nonstarchy fruits and vegetables," says Derderian. "Later, when DeMar reintroduced bread, potatoes and bananas, he was amazed at how fast he could run without tiring."

- 1959. Jock Semple's famous 1967 run-in with Kathrine Switzer wasn't his first. When a man wearing a clown suit joined the 1959 race, Semple "sprinted to the clown and tackled him," Derderian writes.

- 1963. A woman jumped into this Boston. Jane Weinbaum ran the last 10K before police blocked her from finishing.

- 1966. With little fanfare, Roberta Gibb ran 3:27 at Boston a year before Switzer became the poster woman for this cause.

Tip for the Day

Realize that recovery from a hard race typically takes about one day for each mile raced. This means you need about a week to get over a 10K, and need to take only easy runs during that week.

Day 45

Date _____

Plan _____

Training for the Day

Training Session

Type   Long ____   Fast ____   Easy ____   Other (specify) _____

Distance _____   **Time** _____

Pace _____   **Splits** _____ / _____ / _____ / _____ / _____

Effort   Max ____   Hard ____   Moderate ____   Mild ____   Rest ____

Warm-up _____   **Cool-down** _____

Cross-training (specify) _____

Training Conditions

Location _____   **Time of day** _____

People   Trained alone ____   Trained w/partner ____   Trained w/group ____

Terrain _____   **Surface** _____

Temperature ____   **Humidity** ____   **Wind** ____   **Precipitation** _____

Training Grade for the Day

Physical status	A	B	C	D	F
Psychological status	A	B	C	D	F

Comments _____

_____

_____

119

Day 46

Thought for the Day

Other Oldies

Marathoning celebrated the 100th running of Boston in 1996. This makes it by far the oldest marathon in the United States, but many others are showing their age. Fifteen races have lasted 30 years or more, meaning they were in business before running boomed.

In the same year when Boston ran for the 100th time, Yonkers in New York had its 60th running. Western Hemisphere in California would turn 50 in 1997.

The following marathons, listed by birth year, are the most elderly:

Race (City)	Year
BAA (Boston, MA)	1897
Yonkers (NY)	1935
Western Hemisphere (Culver City, CA)	1948
Pike's Peak (Manitou Springs, CO)	1956
Atlantic City (NJ)	1959
Long Island (East Meadow, NY)	1959
Heart of America (Columbia, MO)	1960
Washington's Birthday (Greenbelt, MD)	1962
Equinox (Fairbanks, AK)	1963
Race of Champions (Holyoke, MA)	1963
Atlanta (GA)	1963
Detroit Free Press (MI)	1963
Mardi Gras (New Orleans, LA)	1963
Piedmont Triad (Greensboro, NC)	1965
San Diego (CA)	1965

Tip for the Day

Aside from the speedwork factor, running short races during marathon training supplies an element of excitement that you miss while running alone. Don't deprive yourself of this for these three months.

Day 46

Date _____

Plan _____

Training for the Day

Training Session

Type   Long ____   Fast ____   Easy ____   Other (specify) _____

Distance _____   **Time** _____

Pace _____   **Splits** _____ / _____ / _____ / _____ / _____

Effort   Max ____   Hard ____   Moderate ____   Mild ____   Rest ____

Warm-up _____   **Cool-down** _____

Cross-training (specify) _____

Training Conditions

Location _____   **Time of day** _____

People   Trained alone ____   Trained w/partner ____   Trained w/group ____

Terrain _____   **Surface** _____

Temperature ____   **Humidity** ____   **Wind** ____   **Precipitation** _____

Training Grade for the Day

Physical status   A   B   C   D   F

Psychological status   A   B   C   D   F

Comments _____

_____

_____

Day 47

Thought for the Day

Join the Crowd

"What do you say about the New York City Marathon that hasn't already been said?" I wondered while walking back to my hotel. I wasn't yet thinking what to write but what to tell my wife by phone.

New York is the world's most reported race. Local television covered it live for five hours this year, and highlights would air nationally that afternoon. The *Times* would carry a 22-page special section the next morning.

Before leaving home, I'd read and reviewed the coffee-table book about this marathon. Later the running magazines would all do their annual reports. Over this marathon's life span, the entry list had passed a quarter million. Each runner had a story to tell, and hundreds had told them.

I was late to arrive in New York. I'd waited until the 25th running to join this crowd. Now the race was over for me. After thinking for an hour (the time needed to move from the crowded finish area to the nearby hotel) about what to tell Barbara, my one-sentence summary came out unrehearsed: "It was a once-in-a-lifetime experience."

I meant that both ways. It was an awesome day, unlike any I'd ever known in running and one I'll never forget. And it was an overwhelming day that I never care to repeat.

New York was my largest race ever, and I finished right in the center of its field of almost thirty thousand. This gave me a perfect typical-runner's view of The Race That Fred Built.

Tip for the Day

In place of a short race, insert a speed workout. Total one to three miles (either as a straight run or as interval training) while running at about your current 10K race pace.

Day 47

Date _____

Plan _____

Training for the Day

Training Session

Type   Long ____   Fast ____   Easy ____   Other (specify) _____

Distance _____   **Time** _____

Pace _____   **Splits** _____ / _____ / _____ / _____ / _____

Effort   Max ____   Hard ____   Moderate ____   Mild ____   Rest ____

Warm-up _____   **Cool-down** _____

Cross-training (specify) _____

Training Conditions

Location _____   **Time of day** _____

People   Trained alone ___   Trained w/partner ___   Trained w/group ___

Terrain _____   **Surface** _____

Temperature ____   **Humidity** ____   **Wind** ____   **Precipitation** _____

Training Grade for the Day

Physical status   A   B   C   D   F

Psychological status   A   B   C   D   F

Comments _____

_____

_____

Day 48

Thought for the Day

Running New York City

I knew what to expect from watching and reading about the New York City Marathon for all its years, yet wasn't completely prepared for being in the middle of it. A race this size through a city this size seems unworkable.

Allan Steinfeld and his army of workers somehow make it all work. They see to every runner's needs—physical, logistical, and emotional. But this isn't to say they can satisfy everyone's wishes. Everyone would like to walk to the starting line a few minutes before the gun fires, find a spot on the front row, hit full stride right away, and take a clear path to the finish. You can't do that at New York. In trade for running with this many people, and in front of hundreds of thousands more, you give up personal space and time. This bothers you only if you let it.

A race this big doesn't suit my style of running marathons. That is to line up at the back, start slowly and work my way toward the middle, and take short walks at regular intervals. At New York, this means waiting for miles before starting to move up—and even then doing it only by becoming a zigzagging broken-field runner who risks blind-side blocks. It means risking rear-end collisions when stopping to walk.

I came away with a few bruises, and unavoidably delivered an equal number. I took 15 minutes longer than normal to finish, but it was time well spent. I had to see if all the fuss about New York was justified. And it was. Every runner should have this once-in-a-lifetime experience.

Tip for the Day

Consider running some of your speedwork as intervals—short segments divided by walks or slow runs for recovery. A sample workout: three times one mile, with a five-minute break between miles.

Day 48

Date _____

Plan _____

Training for the Day

Training Session

Type   Long ____   Fast ____   Easy ____   Other (specify) _____

Distance _____   **Time** _____

Pace _____   **Splits** _____ / _____ / _____ / _____ / _____

Effort   Max ____   Hard ____   Moderate ____   Mild ____   Rest ____

Warm-up _____   **Cool-down** _____

Cross-training (specify) _____

Training Conditions

Location _____   **Time of day** _____

People   Trained alone ____   Trained w/partner ____   Trained w/group ____

Terrain _____   **Surface** _____

Temperature ____   **Humidity** ____   **Wind** ____   **Precipitation** _____

Training Grade for the Day

| **Physical status** | A | B | C | D | F |
| **Psychological status** | A | B | C | D | F |

Comments _____

_____

_____

Day 49

Thought for the Day

Get Outta Town

Modern marathoning is largely an urban sport. Big-city races offer the size and services that runners have come to expect. Attractive as going to the country might sound, few runners will go if it means giving up the amenities. Few rural areas have big-bucks sponsors, large volunteer corps, or active publicity machines. So they can't dish out the goodies that attract runners by the thousands.

But if you're looking for a medium-sized (say, more than a thousand entrants) rural marathon (at least 90 percent outside any city's limits) with citylike attractions, the pickings are slim. Only a few events qualify on all counts.

All but one is out west. The exception: Grandma's, which finishes in Duluth each June. The others: Big Sur, an April race ending in Carmel . . . California International, running to Sacramento in December . . . Deseret News, a July race to Salt Lake City . . . Las Vegas, run in February . . . Napa Valley, in March . . . St. George, in October.

All seven marathons follow point-to-point courses. They start in the country and take runners into the host city. A country boy by birth and still one at heart, I've run most of these marathons. But you didn't have to begin as I did to like the country. One of the reasons we all run is to escape the cars, the crowds, and the concrete. We want to get out for a little while where we can feel less citified.

Tip for the Day

Whenever you run a short race or speed workout, warm up for it with at least an easy mile and preferably some "strides"—short runs at the pace at which you intend to train or compete. Cool down with another easy mile or so.

Day 49

Date _____

Plan _____

Training for the Day

Training Session

Type   Long ____   Fast ____   Easy ____   Other (specify) _____

Distance _____   **Time** _____

Pace _____   **Splits** _____ / _____ / _____ / _____ / _____

Effort   Max ____   Hard ____   Moderate ____   Mild ____   Rest ____

Warm-up _____   **Cool-down** _____

Cross-training (specify) _____

Training Conditions

Location _____   **Time of day** _____

People Trained alone ____   Trained w/partner ____   Trained w/group ____

Terrain _____   **Surface** _____

Temperature ____   **Humidity** ____   **Wind** ____   **Precipitation** _____

Training Grade for the Day

Physical status   A   B   C   D   F

Psychological status   A   B   C   D   F

Comments _____

_____

_____

Honolulu is the most international event in the U.S., with 70 percent of its runners coming from Japan.

© Ken Lee

WEEK EIGHT:
Choosing Shoes

Now that you've entered the second half of the program, check yourself out as a marathoner would when the race really begins— just past the halfway point. How do you feel? Any problems with lingering pain, with chronic fatigue? How's your equipment working out? We give special attention in this week's Thoughts to your most important equipment item—the shoes. Choose your program below, assign workouts to the next seven days' diary pages, and add details there for completed training.

Cruiser Program
Big day: semi-long run of eight to nine miles, or half the distance of last week's long one. Run this distance nonstop, with no walking breaks. Run slightly faster than your projected marathon pace.
Other training days: three or four easy runs of 30 to 45 minutes each, with walking breaks optional.
Rest days: two or three with no running, but possibly cross-training.

Pacer Program
Big day: race of 5K to 10K, or fast solo run of one to three miles (may be broken into intervals) at current 10K race pace. Warm up and cool down with easy running.
Other training days: four to five easy runs of 30 to 60 minutes each.
Rest days: one or two with no running, but possibly cross-training.

Racer Program
Long day: long run of 21 to 23 miles, or about a 1-mile increase from your last one. Run about one minute per mile slower than marathon pace.
Fast day: one- to three-mile run at current 10K race pace (this may be broken into shorter intervals that total one to three miles, not counting recovery periods). Warm up and cool down with easy running.
Other training days: four easy runs of 30 to 60 minutes each.
Rest days: one with no running, but possibly cross-training.

Day 50

Thought for the Day

Dressing Down

Jeff Johnson designed many of the shoes that first made Nike a force in the industry. He then retired from Nike in 1983 and moved to New Hampshire to do what he really wanted: coach runners. Since then, Johnson hasn't kept up with the sport's fashion trends. While compiling a recent book, I asked Jeff for his advice on shoe choices.

He claimed to have little to say about shoes because "I am very remote from them these days. For example, I can't discuss the evolution of all-purpose [cross-training] shoes because all of that occurred after I left the industry."

After some prodding, Jeff added, "When people ask me, 'What shoe should I buy?' they assume I have a ready answer on what the best shoe is. I don't. There is no single perfect shoe, for everyone. There is, however, a right shoe for you."

He noted that "today's problem, if it can be called that, is not a shortage of quality shoes but their great abundance—almost an overselection that can confuse even an experienced runner. What you must do is identify your needs and narrow the selection to a group of shoes which would meet those needs."

Now he can say what he couldn't while selling more expensive, ever higher tech shoes: "Wear the least shoe you possibly can. By that, I mean the lightest and cheapest you can tolerate, not the most you can carry or afford. Once a satisfactory choice is identified, stick with it despite the seductive claims of advertising that try to entice you into something new."

Tip for the Day

Ask yourself, how am I adapting to the increased training? Do I feel energetic or lethargic? Am I pain-free or sore from the extra mileage? Have I caught any illnesses related to the extra stress?

Day 50

Date _____

Plan _____

Training for the Day

Training Session

Type   Long ____   Fast ____   Easy ____   Other (specify) _____

Distance _____   **Time** _____

Pace _____   **Splits** _____ / _____ / _____ / _____ / _____

Effort   Max ____   Hard ____   Moderate ____   Mild ____   Rest ____

Warm-up _____   **Cool-down** _____

Cross-training (specify) _____

Training Conditions

Location _____   **Time of day** _____

People   Trained alone ____   Trained w/partner ____   Trained w/group ____

Terrain _____   **Surface** _____

Temperature ____   **Humidity** ____   **Wind** ____   **Precipitation** _____

Training Grade for the Day

Physical status	A	B	C	D	F
Psychological status	A	B	C	D	F

Comments _____

_____

_____

Day 51

Thought for the Day

Views of Shoes

He looked at my feet, not my face, while asking his questions. He stared at the shoes I wore, which weren't the latest style but looked as if they'd come from a discount store. And did.

"What shoes do you prefer?" asked the man at the race clinic in Cedar Rapids, Iowa. "Or are you on contract with a company and have no choice about what to wear?"

I answered his second question first. Except for a few years working with Nike, I've never had to wear a certain brand of shoe. But for a long time, benefactors from various companies had always supplied shoes to test. I took whatever they offered, as long as it worked. I felt little loyalty to any label, only to my feet and legs.

Then my sources of freebies dried up. I resumed buying shoes for the first time since they cost about $20 a pair. Many models now cost $100 or more, and most top $80. None advertised in the running magazines go for less than $50. Yet I still rarely need to pay *more* than $50.

If wearing the latest top-of-the-line styles isn't a requirement, if you only want a simple shoe for basic running, and if you'll accept models marked down because they're outdated or show blemishes, then a $50 shoe will work.

The Cedar Rapids man's other question dealt with preferences. My answers have changed almost totally since last writing shoe reports for *Runner's World* in the 1970s.

Tip for the Day

Check your fatigue level. Long runs are supposed to tire you temporarily, but if the feeling lingers longer than a few days, ease the effort of your next long one by slowing the pace or taking walking breaks.

Day 51

Date _____

Plan _____

Training for the Day

Training Session

Type   Long ____   Fast ____   Easy ____   Other (specify) _____

Distance _____   **Time** _____

Pace _____   **Splits** _____ / _____ / _____ / _____ / _____

Effort   Max ____   Hard ____   Moderate ____   Mild ____   Rest ____

Warm-up _____   **Cool-down** _____

Cross-training (specify) _____

Training Conditions

Location _____   **Time of day** _____

People   Trained alone ____   Trained w/partner ____   Trained w/group ____

Terrain _____   **Surface** _____

Temperature ____   **Humidity** ____   **Wind** ____   **Precipitation** _____

Training Grade for the Day

Physical status	A	B	C	D	F
Psychological status	A	B	C	D	F

Comments _____

_____

_____

Day 52

Thought for the Day

If the Shoe Fits . . .

If asked for footwear advice 20 years ago, I would have said, "Buy the most expensive shoes you can afford. You can't go wrong by paying more, because this model will last you twice as long and give twice the protection of a cheap imitation that's no bargain."

Back then, price correlated almost perfectly with performance of shoes. That's not necessarily so anymore. You may get little more for the extra money than looks. Or you may get more shoe— more padding, support, and bulk—than you really need. My advice now: Buy the least shoe you can safely and comfortably wear, not the most you can afford or can carry.

Stick with the name brands. You're probably safe with any company that goes to the trouble of advertising in running magazines. Each of these companies produces a wide range of models, at widely varying prices to match the needs of runners and their ability to pay.

Choose all-purpose shoes. At these prices, you want the same pair to work for racing and training, on the roads and off. These will be compromise shoes: more substantial than flimsy racers but lighter than the bulkiest trainers.

Find your weaknesses and the shoes that neutralize them. I'm most vulnerable in the heel area, and need shoes that don't irritate the Achilles tendons, that let me go comfortably without socks, and that allow inserts to slip easily under the insoles.

Brands and models change regularly in my lineup. But they all must satisfy old loyalties to the feet and legs, and new ones to the wallet.

Tip for the Day

Check your pain level. Any soreness that lingers from one run to the next requires attention. It's your warning that a small problem could grow into something major if ignored.

Day 52

Date _____

Plan _____

Training for the Day

Training Session

Type   Long ____   Fast ____   Easy ____   Other (specify) _____

Distance _____   **Time** _____

Pace _____   **Splits** _____ / _____ / _____ / _____ / _____

Effort   Max ____   Hard ____   Moderate ____   Mild ____   Rest ____

Warm-up _____   **Cool-down** _____

Cross-training (specify) _____

Training Conditions

Location _____   **Time of day** _____

People   Trained alone ____   Trained w/partner ____   Trained w/group ____

Terrain _____   **Surface** _____

Temperature ____   **Humidity** ____   **Wind** ____   **Precipitation** _____

Training Grade for the Day

Physical status	A	B	C	D	F
Psychological status	A	B	C	D	F

Comments _____

_____

_____

Day 53

Thought for the Day

Old Soft Shoes

It's not enough just to learn from your experiences. You also must file away those lessons for later use.

I once fancied myself as knowing quite a lot about foot types and shoe choices. In my misspent youth, I oversaw the *Runner's World* shoe surveys that caused all the controversy in the 1970s. What I learned from trying to rank shoes 1-2-3 as if they were football teams was that there's no number-one choice for everyone. There's only a best shoe for each of us.

What that might be depends on your foot structure. Faulty feet come in two basic types: floppy and rigid. The first type, which pronates too much, gets most of the press. The other type, which moves too little, gets far less respect.

Foot type dictates shoe choice. Floppy feet need the maximum support that most of today's shoes provide, while rigid feet need maximum cushioning, which is harder to find now. You don't find both features in the same type of shoe.

My feet stand at the far end of the rigidity scale, with arches that look like a McDonald's sign. They loved shoes like the old Tiger Bostons, with their mushy soles and flimsy heel counters. These feet came to tolerate a wide range of modern shoes as my mileage and pace dropped over the years. But when they're hurting, they beg for the relief provided only by the old soft shoes with the cushioning that my rigid arches don't offer.

Tip for the Day

Rule for running with minor aches and pains: If they cause you to limp or if pain increases as you run, stop. But if form is normal and pain eases as you warm up, continue cautiously.

Day 53

Date _____

Plan _____

Training for the Day

Training Session

Type   Long _____   Fast _____   Easy _____   Other (specify) _____

Distance _____   **Time** _____

Pace _____   **Splits** _____ / _____ / _____ / _____ / _____

Effort   Max _____   Hard _____   Moderate _____   Mild _____   Rest _____

Warm-up _____   **Cool-down** _____

Cross-training (specify) _____

Training Conditions

Location _____   **Time of day** _____

People   Trained alone _____   Trained w/partner _____   Trained w/group _____

Terrain _____   **Surface** _____

Temperature _____   **Humidity** _____   **Wind** _____   **Precipitation** _____

Training Grade for the Day

Physical status	A	B	C	D	F
Psychological status	A	B	C	D	F

Comments _____

_____

_____

Day 54

Thought for the Day

What the Doctor Ordered

Dr. Joe Ellis gave me a refresher course in podiatry at just the right time. He writes in the style of James Herriot, the British vet, telling stories about his patients in a book we worked on together titled *Running Injury-Free*.

Dr. Ellis told of a runner named Girard who came to him with a knee injury. "I've had occasional, mild discomfort in this area throughout my four-year running career," said the patient. "But a change of shoes usually solved the problem quickly."

The podiatrist noted that "he'd developed the habit of buying a new pair of running shoes every two months, no matter what the condition of his current shoes. He didn't want to take the chance of having them break down and cause him painful symptoms. When the pain started this time, he again tried switching shoes. Unfortunately, his pains didn't respond. In fact, they worsened."

That's because he chose the wrong shoes for his rigid feet, which absorbed shock poorly and required extra cushioning. Yet he bought a firm, motion-controlling shoe. Ellis said, "It was an easy matter to put him into the correct, softer, slip-lasted shoes without motion-control devices." He ran his first marathon soon afterward.

This story reminded me that I'd recently bought two new pairs of shoes, then suffered heel, knee, and sciatic pains. Both pairs had firmer, dual-density soles and more rigid heel counters than those they replaced. On Ellis's recommendation, I switched to softer shoes. The foot and leg miseries that had hung around for months vanished almost overnight.

Tip for the Day

If you're hurting slightly, use the first mile of the day as your test. Decide only after this warm-up whether or not to complete this day's workout. Sometimes stopping does you more good than continuing.

Day 54

Date _____

Plan _____

Training for the Day

Training Session

Type　　Long ____　Fast ____　Easy ____　Other (specify) _____

Distance _____　**Time** _____

Pace _____　**Splits** _____ / _____ / _____ / _____ / _____

Effort　　Max ____　Hard ____　Moderate ____　Mild ____　Rest ____

Warm-up _____　**Cool-down** _____

Cross-training (specify) _____

Training Conditions

Location _____　**Time of day** _____

People　Trained alone ____　Trained w/partner ____　Trained w/group ____

Terrain _____　**Surface** _____

Temperature ____　**Humidity** ____　**Wind** ____　**Precipitation** _____

Training Grade for the Day

Physical status　　　　　A　　B　　C　　D　　F

Psychological status　　　A　　B　　C　　D　　F

Comments _____

_____

_____

Day 55

Thought for the Day

Shedding Socks

Some items of clothing you think of in pairs. Shorts come with shirts, jackets with long pants, hats with gloves. So too, socks go with shoes. You don't run in one without the other. Not unless you're an iconoclast like Paul Reese. He goes sockless. Before thinking this as odd as wearing shoes without strings, hear him out.

Paul ran across the United States in 1990, when he was 73. Since then, he has crossed most of the remaining states west of the Mississippi. He writes about these treks in his second book, *How the West Was Run*, in which he leaves few experiences unexamined.

"A few times, being sockless," says Paul, "I've been the target of a snide remark like, 'Hey, real macho. No socks.' That's bushwa. Macho has nothing to do with it."

He then gives his rationale for letting nothing come between his shoes and his skin: "The main reason for not wearing socks is that I feel closer to the earth and get a better feel for the road. Hell, I just plain enjoy running more when sockless.

"Another factor: Consider what I save by not buying socks or having to launder them. And, let's face it, modern running shoes are so well made that they are quite comfortable without socks. Yet another reason: It was often my experience as a sock wearer that by slipping or getting twisted they actually *caused* blisters. In more than 5,000 miles of running across states, sockless, I have yet to develop a blister."

Tip for the Day

During times of minor injury, substitute another activity for the scheduled run. Bicycling, swimming, running in water, or walking seldom aggravates the problem but still gives a decent workout.

Day 55

Date _____

Plan _____

Training for the Day

Training Session

Type   Long ____   Fast ____   Easy ____   Other (specify) _____

Distance _____   **Time** _____

Pace _____   **Splits** _____ / _____ / _____ / _____ / _____

Effort   Max ____   Hard ____   Moderate ____   Mild ____   Rest ____

Warm-up _____   **Cool-down** _____

Cross-training (specify) _____

Training Conditions

Location _____   **Time of day** _____

People   Trained alone ____   Trained w/partner ____   Trained w/group ____

Terrain _____   **Surface** _____

Temperature ____   **Humidity** ____   **Wind** ____   **Precipitation** _____

Training Grade for the Day

Physical status   A   B   C   D   F

Psychological status   A   B   C   D   F

Comments _____

_____

_____

Day 56

Thought for the Day

Naked Feet

Hosiers and their advertising claims be damned. I side with Paul Reese, the oldest trans-America runner, on the matter of naked feet.

The practice goes back to my early running, when the only socks available—heavy, baggy sweatsocks—bunched up in your shoes unless you taped them at the ankles. I came to like going sockless for a reason that Paul didn't mention: It gave the illusion of longer, thinner legs, and my stumps needed all the help they could get.

Like him, I got odd looks at the starting line of races. I too heard, "You're running that way? I'd hate to see your feet afterward." They looked no worse then than at the start—and look a lot better now than during the few years I was forced into socks. Those were the low-cut minisocks that came into fashion around 1980. I used them to protect against the orthotics that had come between me and my shoes. This the socks did, but at high cost to skin (blistering) and bone (from slippage at the heel).

Then shoes started coming with removable insoles. Under them went my custom-made inserts, and off came the socks. They've stayed off ever since. My feet give thanks for removing that irritant and for again putting them in closer touch with the earth.

The only downside: Without socks to soak up some of the sweat, the shoes take it all. Left to ripen, they smell like a runner who never showers. Against all advice from manufacturers, I toss my shoes into the washer every few days. It's either that or treat them like a dirty dog who can never come in the house or ride in the car.

Tip for the Day

Treat illnesses with the greatest respect. *Never* run with a fever, and *always* rest a cold during its heaviest phase. Failure to take a few days off can penalize you for several weeks and blow the whole program.

Day 56

Date _____

Plan _____

Training for the Day

Training Session

Type   Long ____   Fast ____   Easy ____   Other (specify) _____

Distance _____   **Time** _____

Pace _____   **Splits** _____ / _____ / _____ / _____ / _____

Effort   Max ____   Hard ____   Moderate ____   Mild ____   Rest ____

Warm-up _____   **Cool-down** _____

Cross-training (specify) _____

Training Conditions

Location _____   **Time of day** _____

People   Trained alone ____   Trained w/partner ____   Trained w/group ____

Terrain _____   **Surface** _____

Temperature ____   **Humidity** ____   **Wind** ____   **Precipitation** _____

Training Grade for the Day

Physical status	A	B	C	D	F
Psychological status	A	B	C	D	F

Comments _____

_____

_____

Joan Benoit Samuelson, who won the first Olympic Marathon for women in 1984, is shown here at Boston nine years later.

WEEK NINE:
Weathering Storms

One month to marathon day! Besides planning your training between now and then, plan your travel. How will you get to the race site, and with whom? When will you arrive there? Where will you stay? Plan also how you'll deal with the weather, which you can't control but can accommodate. Choose your program below, assign workouts to the next seven days' diary pages, and add details there for completed training.

Cruiser Program
Big day: race of five kilometers, or fast solo run of one to three miles. In either case, run at least one minute per mile faster than your projected marathon pace.
Other training days: three or four easy runs of 30 to 45 minutes each, with walking breaks optional.
Rest days: two or three with no running, but possibly cross-training.

Pacer Program
Big day: semi-long run of 9 to 10 miles, or half the distance of your last long one. Run this distance nonstop, at your projected marathon pace or slightly faster.
Other training days: four to five easy runs of 30 to 60 minutes each.
Rest days: one or two with no running, but possibly cross-training.

Racer Program
Long day: semi-long run of 10 to 11 miles, or approximately half the distance of last week's long one. Run at your projected marathon pace or slightly faster.
Fast day: race of 5K to 10K, or one- to three-mile run at current 10K race pace (this may be broken into shorter intervals that total one to three miles, not counting recovery periods). Warm up and cool down with easy running.
Other training days: four easy runs of 30 to 60 minutes each.
Rest days: one with no running, but possibly cross-training.

Day 57

Thought for the Day

Weather Wimp

Pardon me if I sound a bit defensive on this issue. Sure, I left the Midwest for two reasons—winter and summer, each of which lasts about 5-1/2 months. But don't call me a weather wimp for living the past 30 years on the West Coast, which gets all the good days that my old home misses.

My defenses came up when a letter appeared in *Runner's World*. A woman from Dallas wrote, "After reading the column in which Henderson dismissed the use of sunglasses by runners, I can only assume that he has never tried to run in the Texas sun."

What raised my hackles in this letter was its implication of weather wimpiness. Readers must wonder how anyone from Out There could possibly understand how they live. We don't have real weather on the Coast, they think, only a benign climate.

OK, so we don't have tornadoes or hurricanes. It doesn't get too cold and slick for running in winter, or too hot and humid in summer. Granted, it rains a lot in the Northwest. But that keeps the grass green all winter and keeps too many sun lovers from moving here.

The West Coast is climatically mild, but only if you're talking about the 100 miles nearest the Pacific. Venture a little farther inland, though, and you'll find weather in the extreme. The hottest run I've ever taken—at 111 degrees—was in a California desert. The worst I've ever been snowbound was at Lake Tahoe, which straddles the California-Nevada border.

No runner, regardless of hometown, can escape the extremes all the time. Running in them makes the good days feel better.

Tip for the Day

Select a marathon where weather is likely to be favorable. The kindest days for a marathoner feature temperatures around 50, with calm winds and cloudy skies.

Day 57

Date _____

Plan _____

Training for the Day

Training Session

Type   Long ____   Fast ____   Easy ____   Other (specify) _____

Distance _____   **Time** _____

Pace _____   **Splits** _____ / _____ / _____ / _____ / _____

Effort   Max ____   Hard ____   Moderate ____   Mild ____   Rest ____

Warm-up _____   **Cool-down** _____

Cross-training (specify) _____

Training Conditions

Location _____   **Time of day** _____

People   Trained alone ____   Trained w/partner ____   Trained w/group ____

Terrain _____   **Surface** _____

Temperature ____   **Humidity** ____   **Wind** ____   **Precipitation** _____

Training Grade for the Day

Physical status   A   B   C   D   F

Psychological status   A   B   C   D   F

Comments _____

_____

_____

Day 58

Thought for the Day

Days Like This

I may live in the Far West but I don't stay here all the time. My travels take me to the extremes, such as running at a minus-66 windchill in Chicago . . . wading knee-deep through monsoon rains in Honolulu . . . eyelids freezing shut during a snowstorm in Iowa . . . going out at midnight in Memphis, where the temperature still topped 90 degrees and the humidity was thick enough to chew.

My theory, after running in—and running from—bad weather for lots of years, is that the extremes aren't the big problem. We run eagerly on these days so we can brag about it later. The bigger problem is with borderline-bad days. Two Boston Marathons, in consecutive years, stand as examples.

The first, the 1976 "run for the hoses," was the hottest in Boston's history. The starting-line temperature officially read 97, but the unshaded road was much hotter. We knew we couldn't run very fast on a day like that, so we forgot about setting PRs and just did the best we could under those conditions. Those of us who were there still brag about challenging that heat and surviving it.

The next year's Boston temperature was 20 degrees lower but still too warm. Never have I seen so many looks of defeat (or worn a darker one myself) at the finish line. This borderline-bad day was more troubling than the extreme heat of the year before because it let us hold fast to our goals and pacing schemes. We tried to beat this heat, and failed.

Tip for the Day

You can't pick a perfect marathon day but must take what comes that day. Prepare for whatever it might bring by training long or fast as scheduled, regardless of the day's conditions.

Day 58

Date _____

Plan _____

Training for the Day

Training Session

Type   Long ____   Fast ____   Easy ____   Other (specify) _____

Distance _____   **Time** _____

Pace _____   **Splits** _____ / _____ / _____ / _____ / _____

Effort   Max ____   Hard ____   Moderate ____   Mild ____   Rest ____

Warm-up _____   **Cool-down** _____

Cross-training (specify) _____

Training Conditions

Location _____   **Time of day** _____

People   Trained alone ____   Trained w/partner ____   Trained w/group ____

Terrain _____   **Surface** _____

Temperature ____   **Humidity** ____   **Wind** ____   **Precipitation** _____

Training Grade for the Day

Physical status	A	B	C	D	F
Psychological status	A	B	C	D	F

Comments _____

_____

_____

Day 59

Thought for the Day

Rain Man

I confess to a fondness for rainy runs that isn't widely shared, or even well understood outside the soggy Pacific Northwest. This comes partly from living here now and partly from good memories of old rains.

In Iowa boyhood summers long ago, I prayed for rain to break the hot spells. Thunderstormy days—and those blessed hours right afterward when the front had passed and left cooler, fresher air—were the only ones fit for long runs.

Eugene, Oregon, is home now. It's known as the running capital, but it's equally a *raining* capital. I don't mind, since I've learned to appreciate the subtle beauties of soggy days.

My first marathon came in near-freezing drizzle at Boston. It numbed me from the waist up but left the legs to work just fine. I never again ran faster than that day, and I'd take a dozen of those days over the near 100-degree day at Boston in 1976.

Heat is the runner's common enemy. The Long Beach Marathon once moved its marathon from May to February after weathering a five-year streak of warm racedays. After this move, the event faced an unusual threat for southern California: rain. This prediction deluged the marathon's office with questions: "Will the race still be held?" "What should I wear to protect myself from the rain?" "How will the bad conditions affect my performance?"

What to do about rain? Hope and pray for a light misting of it on an otherwise mild, calm raceday. It's nature's perfect cooling system.

Tip for the Day

View the bad-weather training days as opportunities rather than penalties. They give you the chance to test your clothing, shoes, pacing, and toughness under the most trying conditions.

Day 59

Date _____

Plan _____

Training for the Day

Training Session

Type   Long ____   Fast ____   Easy ____   Other (specify) _____

Distance _____   **Time** _____

Pace _____   **Splits** _____ / _____ / _____ / _____ / _____

Effort   Max ____   Hard ____   Moderate ____   Mild ____   Rest ____

Warm-up _____   **Cool-down** _____

Cross-training (specify) _____

Training Conditions

Location _____   **Time of day** _____

People   Trained alone ____   Trained w/partner ____   Trained w/group ____

Terrain _____   **Surface** _____

Temperature ____   **Humidity** ____   **Wind** ____   **Precipitation** _____

Training Grade for the Day

Physical status	A	B	C	D	F
Psychological status	A	B	C	D	F

Comments _____

_____

_____

Day 60

Thought for the Day

Heated Battles

You don't just wake up and decide, "I'm going to run a marathon today." You can do that with a short race but not a long one. The longer the race, the longer its planning and training phase. And after all that preparation, months for a marathon, you still don't know how the race will go.

In a 10K, you can predict your finish time within a minute or so. Weather will affect your time only within that narrow range. If race morning looks really bad, you can say, "Not today. I'll try again next week."

You can't do that with a marathon. You can't wake up on raceday and decide *not* to run. You've invested too much. You've trained too long for this day. Even if you haven't traveled far to the race, there isn't another like it this close next week.

Scheduling your marathon months in advance is a gamble. Sometimes you lose. The losses multiply with the distance. Conditions that cause a slow finish in the short race can force a *no*-finish, or worse, in the long one.

Heat worries everyone the most. Think how you'd feel if a marathon day dawned hot, messed up your racing plans, and caused you to hurt more for a PW than you would have for a PR. Now think how race directors react to the heat. They've planned for this day even longer than you have, and they've invested more in its outcome—only to have their hopes for all of you melt into fears.

Tip for the Day

Assume that the apparent temperature will jump by 20 degrees when you start to run. A 20-degree day, for instance, will warm up quickly to feel like a tolerable 40.

Day 60

Date _____

Plan _____

Training for the Day

Training Session

Type　　Long ____　Fast ____　Easy ____　Other (specify) _____

Distance _____　**Time** _____

Pace _____　**Splits** _____ / _____ / _____ / _____ / _____

Effort　　Max ____　Hard ____　Moderate ____　Mild ____　Rest ____

Warm-up _____　**Cool-down** _____

Cross-training (specify) _____

Training Conditions

Location _____　**Time of day** _____

People　Trained alone ____　Trained w/partner ____　Trained w/group ____

Terrain _____　**Surface** _____

Temperature ____　**Humidity** ____　**Wind** ____　**Precipitation** _____

Training Grade for the Day

Physical status　　　　　　A　　　B　　　C　　　D　　　F

Psychological status　　　　A　　　B　　　C　　　D　　　F

Comments _____

_____

_____

Day 61

Thought for the Day

Hot Times

You worry on a hot raceday about one runner whose efforts you think you can control. Race directors worry about *all* the runners who might lose control on a hot day.

Joe Carlson directed the Long Beach Marathon as his full-time job. He once ran in an Olympic Trial but never worried as much as a runner as he did as a director. And he never had more reason to sweat than in the race's hottest year.

Long Beach fried in 102-degree heat the afternoon before the race. Carlson said then, "The forecast is for cooler weather tomorrow morning. But if it gets this hot again, we'll have to consider shortening or even canceling the marathon."

That would be terrible for the four-thousand-plus runners who'd trained for it and traveled a long way to be here. But Carlson said, "It would be a greater potential tragedy to put everyone in a dangerous situation that we could have avoided."

The marathon's medical adviser set temperature/humidity limits for ending the race early and for calling it off. Neither was reached, though the temperature 2-1/2 hours into the race hit 80 degrees and it topped 90 at 4 hours.

Carlson awaited casualty reports. To his relief, the medics treated only one heat injury serious enough to require hospital care. Ninety percent of the starters finished, a near-normal total. The times didn't show it, but this was a day for heroic efforts—from the 9 runners in every 10 who ran wisely enough to finish, and even from the other one who was wise enough not to push too far.

Tip for the Day

On cold and windy days, run the worst part first. On an out-and-back course, run the "out" portion into the wind. You'll instantly feel better after turning around and starting back with a tailwind.

Day 61

Date _____

Plan _____

Training for the Day

Training Session

Type   Long ____   Fast ____   Easy ____   Other (specify) _____

Distance _____   **Time** _____

Pace _____   **Splits** _____ / _____ / _____ / _____ / _____

Effort   Max ____   Hard ____   Moderate ____   Mild ____   Rest ____

Warm-up _____   **Cool-down** _____

Cross-training (specify) _____

Training Conditions

Location _____   **Time of day** _____

People Trained alone ____   Trained w/partner ____   Trained w/group ____

Terrain _____   **Surface** _____

Temperature ____   **Humidity** ____   **Wind** ____   **Precipitation** _____

Training Grade for the Day

Physical status   A   B   C   D   F

Psychological status   A   B   C   D   F

Comments _____

_____

_____

Day 62

Thought for the Day

Winter Is Cool

I'm just in from a two-hour run. It's my longest this year, on the coldest day of the year. Well, the year is still only three days old. But two hours is as far as I'll run alone and today's temperature is as low as it will go all year.

The thermometer reads a little below freezing, and a stiff wind chills that reading to zero. This passes for a serious winter day in Oregon. I didn't see another runner all morning. This doesn't surprise me, because the local running traffic always drops with the temperature. Yet here I was running in shorts (long ones, to be sure, but still bare from the knees down). I couldn't wipe the goofy grin off my face. Now I'm thinking, "Winter is cool."

I'm not so weird as to call winter my favorite season. But none of the others has served me better, longer. Winter first made me a runner. Without it, I might not be running in *any* season now.

I wasn't much of a runner through 1-1/2 years of high school. I was an all-sports athlete who ran only during spring track season. Fall was for football, winter for basketball, summer for swimming. No one at my school ever thought to run out of season.

But neither was anyone ever more poorly endowed to play basketball. Five-feet-five, with a poor shooting eye and a minuscule vertical jump, I never rose higher than 13th man on a 14-member team. Twelve players suited up for games. Seeing no chance even to ride the bench, I became a winter runner by default.

Tip for the Day

On the hottest days, figure the "20-degree rule" will work against you. A temperature in the 80s will soon feel like 100-plus, so dress and pace yourself for the higher reading.

Day 62

Date _____

Plan _____

Training for the Day

Training Session

Type Long ____ Fast ____ Easy ____ Other (specify) _____

Distance _____ **Time** _____

Pace _____ **Splits** _____ / _____ / _____ / _____ / _____

Effort Max ____ Hard ____ Moderate ____ Mild ____ Rest ____

Warm-up _____ **Cool-down** _____

Cross-training (specify) _____

Training Conditions

Location _____ **Time of day** _____

People Trained alone ____ Trained w/partner ____ Trained w/group ____

Terrain _____ **Surface** _____

Temperature ____ **Humidity** ____ **Wind** ____ **Precipitation** _____

Training Grade for the Day

Physical status   A   B   C   D   F

Psychological status   A   B   C   D   F

Comments _____

_____

_____

Day 63

Thought for the Day

Snow Business

The coach didn't try to talk me out of quitting the high school basketball team. But Mr. Roe did ask, "What do you plan to do between now and track season?" He coached all sports and expected all his boys to stay in shape all year.

I didn't come to him with a plan but made one up on the spot. "Uh, maybe I could start training early for track."

"Where?" the coach wondered. I told him right here in the gym. He scowled at that answer and said, "Well OK, but don't get in the way of our practices here."

My first day as an out-of-season runner, I rushed a mile before the basketball team took the floor. Seventy left turns blistered me badly. "Winter can't be any worse than this," I thought. The next day, I ran out into the coldest month and stayed outside the rest of that winter.

That track season, my mile time dropped by more than 20 seconds. I placed in the state meet as a sophomore. Nothing hooks a kid quicker on a sport than his first success. This was my first taste of it as a runner—or as an athlete, for that matter.

I imagined then that hard work and a talent for the sport had led to this breakthrough. Now I know it was neither. My workload was laughable by today's standards. I averaged less than 10 miles a week that winter. My talent was nothing special. In any random group of 10 teenagers at the time, 7 would have been stronger and 3 faster.

My edge—my only one—was winter. You don't need to do much to get a jump on people who aren't moving.

Tip for the Day

Quit complaining about the weather. The wind won't die, rain won't stop, and temperature won't shift as a favor to you. Adapt your training to the conditions and take pride in accepting them on their terms.

Day 63

Date _____

Plan _____

Training for the Day

Training Session

Type   Long ____   Fast ____   Easy ____   Other (specify) _____

Distance _____   **Time** _____

Pace _____   **Splits** _____ / _____ / _____ / _____ / _____

Effort   Max ____   Hard ____   Moderate ____   Mild ____   Rest ____

Warm-up _____   **Cool-down** _____

Cross-training (specify) _____

Training Conditions

Location _____   **Time of day** _____

People   Trained alone ____   Trained w/partner ____   Trained w/group ____

Terrain _____   **Surface** _____

Temperature ____   **Humidity** ____   **Wind** ____   **Precipitation** _____

Training Grade for the Day

Physical status   A   B   C   D   F

Psychological status   A   B   C   D   F

Comments _____

_____

_____

The Chicago Marathon typifies the city-wide events that sprung up throughout the U.S. and around the world in the 1970s and '80s.

WEEK TEN:
Peaking Out

All programs peak this week, with the longest run of this training period. Distances reach at least 18 miles, or about two-thirds of a marathon. But it's strongly recommended that first-time marathoners train at least 20 miles once. This is a major mental hurdle, and once cleared it gives the confidence needed to cover the remaining distance on raceday. Choose your program below, assign workouts to the next seven days' diary pages, and add details there for completed training.

Cruiser Program
Big day: long run of 18 to 20 miles, or about a 2-mile increase from your last one. Mix running and walking while covering the distance no faster than your projected marathon pace.
Other training days: three or four easy runs of 30 to 45 minutes each, with walking breaks optional.
Rest days: two or three with no running, but possibly cross-training.

Pacer Program
Big day: long run of 20 to 22 miles, or about a 2-mile increase from your last one. Walking breaks optional. Run about one minute per mile slower than your projected marathon pace.
Other training days: four to five easy runs of 30 to 60 minutes each.
Rest days: one or two with no running, but possibly cross-training.

Racer Program
Long day: long run of 22 to 24 miles, or about a 1-mile increase from your last one. Run about one minute per mile slower than marathon pace.
Fast day: one- to three-mile run at current 10K race pace (this may be broken into shorter intervals that total one to three miles, not counting recovery periods). Warm up and cool down with easy running.
Other training days: four easy runs of 30 to 60 minutes each.
Rest days: one with no running, but possibly cross-training.

Day 64

Thought for the Day

Longer Days Ahead

Let's lighten up on the Chinese women. For today, let's give full value to their world-leading times and credit them to careful selection and hard work. Accepting all that, we still have a problem. It's not with the Chinese but with the runners who may now try to imitate them in hopes of achieving similar results.

This is a copycat sport. Runners mimic the training of the current world leaders. They did it with the intervals of Emil Zatopek and Roger Bannister, and with the mileage of Peter Snell and Derek Clayton. They'll now imitate the Chinese women.

The trouble is, we don't really know what they're doing. All we know is what we read, and most of that is either misleading or exaggerated. Forget about magic potions made from worms and turtles. Forget too about running like a deer or ostrich. Forget even about the rumors of their juicing up on illicit substances.

The Chinese women are fast because of their training. But how do they train? Probably not the "marathon every day" that we've been led to believe. Much may have been lost—or should we say *gained*?—in the translation from practice to print. And believing what we've read could prove dangerous to any runner who tries to carry training to these extreme lengths.

Tip for the Day

Prepare for the most important run of this training program: your longest (and in fact final long one). It most closely resembles the marathon itself, and you run it three weeks before raceday.

Day 64

Date _____

Plan _____

Training for the Day

Training Session

Type   Long ____   Fast ____   Easy ____   Other (specify) _____

Distance _____   **Time** _____

Pace _____   **Splits** _____ / _____ / _____ / _____ / _____

Effort   Max ____   Hard ____   Moderate ____   Mild ____   Rest ____

Warm-up _____   **Cool-down** _____

Cross-training (specify) _____

Training Conditions

Location _____   **Time of day** _____

People   Trained alone ____   Trained w/partner ____   Trained w/group ____

Terrain _____   **Surface** _____

Temperature ____   **Humidity** ____   **Wind** ____   **Precipitation** _____

Training Grade for the Day

Physical status   A   B   C   D   F

Psychological status   A   B   C   D   F

Comments _____

_____

_____

Day 65

Thought for the Day

Mileage Mania

When Wang Junxia won the 1993 World Championships 10,000 (in which she later set the world record, plus the 3,000 mark), she said through an interpreter, "During the winter preparation for this season, I ran 30 to 40 kilometers [18 to 25 miles] daily."

Marathon historian Dr. David Martin writes, "With a day's passage of time, that press quote underwent an evolution. 'Running 30 to 40 kilometers a day during the winter' soon became 'running the equivalent of a marathon a day,' which became 'running an actual marathon nonstop every day.' "

In fact, Martin says the Chinese probably were dividing their distance into two or three runs. Averaging 35K a day would put them at about 150-mile weeks. That total is still impressive, but not unprecedented.

"Some have said this means Western runners will have to work harder," writes Jeff Hollobaugh in *Track & Field News*. "They've forgotten that Western runners have already tried it . . . with mixed results."

The mix was some success and many breakdowns. For instance, renowned 200-mile-a-week trainer Derek Clayton broke two world marathon records and endured four times as many surgeries.

Reports on Chinese mileage feed the simplistic notion that more—whether it be more distance or more speed—is better. Runners everywhere have a long history of believing in it and suffering for it. The Chinese women have set in motion another escalation of training distances. Even if they aren't running a marathon a day, others will think they are and will try it at their peril.

Tip for the Day

Give yourself a mini-taper before the longest run. Rest up for it by keeping the last few runs quite easy and possibly substituting a day of rest for one of the easier runs.

Day 65

Date _____

Plan _____

Training for the Day

Training Session

Type   Long _____   Fast _____   Easy _____   Other (specify) _____

Distance _____   **Time** _____

Pace _____   **Splits** _____ / _____ / _____ / _____ / _____

Effort   Max _____   Hard _____   Moderate _____   Mild _____   Rest _____

Warm-up _____   **Cool-down** _____

Cross-training (specify) _____

Training Conditions

Location _____   **Time of day** _____

People   Trained alone _____   Trained w/partner _____   Trained w/group _____

Terrain _____   **Surface** _____

Temperature _____   **Humidity** _____   **Wind** _____   **Precipitation** _____

Training Grade for the Day

Physical status   A   B   C   D   F

Psychological status   A   B   C   D   F

Comments _____

_____

_____

Day 66

Thought for the Day

Long Letters

I spoke my piece in magazine columns about the recommended length of long runs (with the same advice given throughout this book). Then several readers had their say, with little further comment from me.

The more traditional among them thought my recommended training distances stopped short of the lengths needed. But others said I went too far.

I heard from one woman in Canada who completed a marathon with *no* training. On the day before the event, she let a friend talk her into accompanying him. A man from California told me about training only once a week. His longest run before a completed marathon was 13 miles.

Les Smith, director of the Portland Marathon, reported his unusual training approach: "After running marathons semi-seriously for several years, I started to do crazy things in the mid-1980s. I would do the New York City event, then not run a step until I started Seattle [about a month later]. No training—except golf.

"Now I run New York with ever-young Mavis Lindgren [in her late 80s]. Great excuse to start early with the Achilles Track Club. My last 'training run' for this outing was walking 36 holes of golf on the Duke University course, where I played as an undergraduate."

Smith wrote, "I'm headed to London. My wife said, 'What are you going to do this year? Mavis is not going with you.' Maybe the weather will get really good, and I can play lots of golf before the marathon."

Tip for the Day

Make sure you get your drinks during the longest training run. Scout the course in advance for drink stops. If you don't find enough of them, stash bottles of your favorite fluid along the route.

Day 66

Date _____

Plan _____

Training for the Day

Training Session

Type   Long ____   Fast ____   Easy ____   Other (specify) _____

Distance _____   **Time** _____

Pace _____   **Splits** _____ / _____ / _____ / _____ / _____

Effort   Max ____   Hard ____   Moderate ____   Mild ____   Rest ____

Warm-up _____   **Cool-down** _____

Cross-training (specify) _____

Training Conditions

Location _____   **Time of day** _____

People   Trained alone ____   Trained w/partner ____   Trained w/group ____

Terrain _____   **Surface** _____

Temperature ____   **Humidity** ____   **Wind** ____   **Precipitation** _____

Training Grade for the Day

Physical status   A   B   C   D   F

Psychological status   A   B   C   D   F

Comments _____

_____

_____

Day 67

Thought for the Day

Run Long and Prosper

Some marathoners practice minimalist training—much less than I'd ever propose. Some think my recommendations don't go far enough. This week, I give space for rebuttals.

Bill Harkins, who runs with a Kansas City-based group called Big Miles Training, wrote to me after I gave the mileage advice that you find in this book. "While agreeing that running the full distance in training for a marathon is a lot of work," said Harkins, "I disagree that it takes any of the mystery (or fear) out of the actual event.

"Big Miles has a very high completion rate for those who train for their first marathon under its program. David Virtue, our director, believes in working up to the full 26 miles in training—even a little more if one can handle that. Going to the starting line after you've already gone the distance gives a tremendous psychological advantage."

Harkins noted that training for a marathon and running the race will always be worlds apart: "There's little pressure in training. No PRs are at stake, no medals lost if you fall a mile short that day. There are no butterflies in your stomach in training, wondering if you'll make it through.

"All of these come with the actual marathon. I don't think training up to the distance diminishes the event in any way. I believe I will always go to the line a little afraid. I'll always wonder what sort of joy or despair each marathon will bring, and will forever be in awe that I'm there at all."

Tip for the Day

Cruisers, consider eating on the run—especially if your marathon will last four hours or more. The most practical food is a sports bar, cut into small pieces and carried in a baggie. Practice eating on the longest training run.

Day 67

Date _____

Plan _____

Training for the Day

Training Session

Type   Long ____   Fast ____   Easy ____   Other (specify) _____

Distance _____   **Time** _____

Pace _____   **Splits** _____ / _____ / _____ / _____ / _____

Effort   Max ____   Hard ____   Moderate ____   Mild ____   Rest ____

Warm-up _____   **Cool-down** _____

Cross-training (specify) _____

Training Conditions

Location _____   **Time of day** _____

People   Trained alone ____   Trained w/partner ____   Trained w/group ____

Terrain _____   **Surface** _____

Temperature ____   **Humidity** ____   **Wind** ____   **Precipitation** _____

Training Grade for the Day

Physical status   A   B   C   D   F

Psychological status   A   B   C   D   F

Comments _____

_____

_____

Day 68

Thought for the Day

True Training

A couple of years ago, I had the pleasure of getting to know dozens of runners and their training habits. While digging through their questionnaires for the book *Road Racers & Their Training*, I wondered how I'd answer the same questions. How would I introduce myself as I've done for them at the top of their stories?

I'd be tempted to add many disclaimers, as Hal Higdon did. He says his approach has changed too much through the years to call anything typical. "How can I summarize my training habits in the answers to a half-dozen questions occupying two sides of a single sheet of paper?" Higdon wrote in his *National Masters News* column. "My training rarely remains the same week to week, or year to year.

"I shift and sway, not from indecision but because my goals change. One season, I might be focused on a marathon. Another, my attention might be drawn to the track. Or I may be taking a mental and physical break from the stress of either effort."

Higdon said he "found it hard to fulfill the request to offer a typical week of training." This said, Higdon selected a week. He let it stand as an example of what he did once. It might not have been "typical," but it was a true snapshot from his training life.

That's what I wanted. Not what the runners hope to do or plan to do (or even advise others to do), but what they themselves really have done.

How would you describe your running in the fewest words? How would you highlight your running-life story in a paragraph?

Tip for the Day

Pacers and Racers, extend your longest training run to marathon length. Try to train as much *time* as you expect the marathon to take, even while going less than 26.2 miles because of the slower training pace.

Day 68

Date _____

Plan _____

Training for the Day

Training Session

Type   Long ____   Fast ____   Easy ____   Other (specify) _____

Distance _____   **Time** _____

Pace _____   **Splits** _____ / _____ / _____ / _____ / _____

Effort   Max ____   Hard ____   Moderate ____   Mild ____   Rest ____

Warm-up _____   **Cool-down** _____

Cross-training (specify) _____

Training Conditions

Location _____   **Time of day** _____

People   Trained alone ____   Trained w/partner ____   Trained w/group ____

Terrain _____   **Surface** _____

Temperature ____   **Humidity** ____   **Wind** ____   **Precipitation** _____

Training Grade for the Day

Physical status	A	B	C	D	F
Psychological status	A	B	C	D	F

Comments _____

_____

_____

Day 69

Thought for the Day

My Miles

While compiling the book *Road Racers & Their Training*, I couldn't resist summarizing myself in the same way. Try it yourself:

Intro: We get about 10 years of racing improvement, Dr. Joan Ullyot once wrote. She made this observation about 10 years too late for me. Without knowing why until later, my best times fit neatly into a decade—beginning in the summer of 1960 when I adopted the long distances, and ending in spring 1970 when a new job drew attention away from my racing.

Bio: Born June 3, 1943, at Peoria, Illinois. Now lives in Eugene, Oregon. 5'5", 130 pounds. Married, three children. Occupation: writer-editor. Began racing in 1958. Self-coached.

Best times: Mile, 4:18 (1964); 5K, 15:42 (1961); 10K, 33:39 (1969); 10 miles, 57:20 (1968); marathon, 2:49:48 (1967).

Training plan: After converting to longer and slower running (what came to be known as LSD) in 1966, and for many years thereafter, the plan was simple: run about an hour most days, with an occasional jump to two hours or more—averaging 7:00 to 7:30 per mile. The almost-weekly races, at widely ranging distances, were the only speedwork.

Sample week of 60 miles from February 1967, about two months before setting marathon PR. Sunday—7 miles, 7:10 pace. Monday—8 miles, 7:15 pace. Tuesday—7 miles, 7:35 pace. Wednesday—6 miles, 7:20 pace. Thursday—8 miles, 7:20 pace. Friday—9 miles, 7:15 pace. Saturday—indoor mile race, 4:37.

Favorite workout: One-hour run at a relaxed pace. This was the first choice almost 30 years ago. Still is.

Tip for the Day

Look how far you've come since the first week of this marathon program. The distance of your long run has jumped by more than 50 percent.

Day 69

Date _____

Plan _____

Training for the Day

Training Session

Type   Long ____   Fast ____   Easy ____   Other (specify) _____

Distance _____   **Time** _____

Pace _____   **Splits** _____ / _____ / _____ / _____ / _____

Effort   Max ____   Hard ____   Moderate ____   Mild ____   Rest ____

Warm-up _____   **Cool-down** _____

Cross-training (specify) _____

Training Conditions

Location _____   **Time of day** _____

People   Trained alone ____   Trained w/partner ____   Trained w/group ____

Terrain _____   **Surface** _____

Temperature ____   **Humidity** ____   **Wind** ____   **Precipitation** _____

Training Grade for the Day

Physical status   A   B   C   D   F

Psychological status   A   B   C   D   F

Comments _____

_____

_____

Day 70

Thought for the Day

What Now?

Calls like this always come before marathons. They scheduled a race and trained for it, and now they're hurt. They call to say, "I don't want to miss it. What can I do to salvage this race?"

Most of them have only their running to blame—the old too-much, too-soon syndrome. Bruce Alexander was different. His injury was accidental, the result of a skiing mishap, and his marathon was now less than two months away. "Before the injury," he said, "I went 25 miles in training. Now I can barely go 1 mile. What are my chances of running the marathon?"

I based my advice on no direct experience with this condition, but on running into, with, through, and away from injuries of many other types. In general, I follow two rules:

- If running causes you to limp and the pain gets worse as you go, stop! You're aggravating the problem.
- If your gait smooths out as you go and the pain diminishes, continue gingerly. You're probably not doing further damage.

Plan to run a single mile. You'll know by then whether to go on or quit for the day.

"If you baby your current injury, it *might* get better," I told Dr. Alexander. "If it does, you can still run your marathon." He trained as pain allowed, then ran-walked the marathon much slower than planned but finished it. He could still tap the fitness that allowed him to run those 25 miles two months earlier.

We spend a long time building up the ability to go long. It doesn't suddenly desert us.

Tip for the Day

Where, you ask, do the extra miles come from if your longest training run stops at four or more miles short of the marathon? Trust the magic of raceday excitement to carry you the extra distance.

Day 70

Date _____

Plan _____

Training for the Day

Training Session

Type   Long ____   Fast ____   Easy ____   Other (specify) _____

Distance _____   **Time** _____

Pace _____   **Splits** _____ / _____ / _____ / _____ / _____

Effort   Max ____   Hard ____   Moderate ____   Mild ____   Rest ____

Warm-up _____   **Cool-down** _____

Cross-training (specify) _____

Training Conditions

Location _____   **Time of day** _____

People   Trained alone ____   Trained w/partner ____   Trained w/group ___

Terrain _____   **Surface** _____

Temperature ____   **Humidity** ____   **Wind** ____   **Precipitation** _____

Training Grade for the Day

Physical status   A   B   C   D   F

Psychological status   A   B   C   D   F

Comments _____

_____

_____

© Rick Davis

Nowhere will runners find a more beautiful meeting of land and water than on the course of the Big Sur Marathon.

WEEK ELEVEN:
Getting Around

Your normal training ends this week, and it won't resume until well after the marathon. Think now, long before you journey to the race city, about the course you'll travel once you get there. Most important: How hilly is it, where are those hills, and how do you plan to deal with them? Choose your program below, assign workouts to the next seven days' diary pages, and add details there for completed training.

Cruiser Program
Big day: semi-long run of 9 to 10 miles, or half the distance of last week's long one. Run this distance nonstop, with no walking breaks. Run slightly faster than your projected marathon pace.
Other training days: three or four easy runs of 30 to 45 minutes each, with walking breaks optional.
Rest days: two or three with no running, but possibly cross-training.

Pacer Program
Big day: race of 5K to 10K, or semi-long run of 10 to 11 miles, half of last week's long one, nonstop at your projected marathon pace or slightly faster.
Other training days: four to five easy runs of 30 to 60 minutes each.
Rest days: one or two with no running, but possibly cross-training.

Racer Program
Long day: semi-long run of 11 to 12 miles, or half the distance of last week's long one. Run at your projected marathon pace or slightly faster.
Fast day: race of 5K to 10K, or one- to three-mile run at current 10K race pace (this may be broken into shorter intervals that total one to three miles, not counting recovery periods). Warm up and cool down with easy running.
Other training days: four easy runs of 30 to 60 minutes each.
Rest days: one with no running, but possibly cross-training.

Day 71

Thought for the Day

Uphill Battles

Anyone who schedules a marathon should be required to run the course before asking others to do it. That way we'd be spared insults such as uphill finishes.

Runners wouldn't design that type of course if they had to use it themselves, or if they honored the wishes of those who did. Runners don't flock to marathons that finish uphill. (Quick, name a large one with a significant climb at the end.) It's bad enough that all marathons *feel* uphill at the end without actually making them so. We complain about stepping up on curbs in the late miles; don't ask us to climb real hills.

Mercifully few marathons require it. Most of those with notorious hills—Boston, Big Sur, St. George—tilt downward to their finish lines. Even Pike's Peak, the U.S. marathon that climbs highest, ends on a steep descent for half its distance.

Obviously the most famous race of all, a direct descendant from the original, doesn't care what its runners think or feel. The wants and needs of athletes usually come last in the scheduling and layout of Olympic Marathons.

For one thing, marathoners prefer not to run races this long in the dead of summer. Their normally cool-weather sport is, at best, a poor fit with the Summer Games. Schedulers add to the burden of out-of-season racing by choosing steamy cities like Barcelona and Atlanta, then adding the insult of an uphill finish. That's not what runners would choose if they had a vote.

Tip for the Day

Make final plans for race weekend, which is now less than three weeks away. Know how you'll get to the race city, when you'll arrive, and where you'll stay. Have the necessary reservations in hand.

Day 71

Date _____

Plan _____

Training for the Day

Training Session

Type   Long ____   Fast ____   Easy ____   Other (specify) _____

Distance _____   **Time** _____

Pace _____   **Splits** _____ / _____ / _____ / _____ / _____

Effort   Max ____   Hard ____   Moderate ____   Mild ____   Rest ____

Warm-up _____   **Cool-down** _____

Cross-training (specify) _____

Training Conditions

Location _____   **Time of day** _____

People   Trained alone ____   Trained w/partner ____   Trained w/group ____

Terrain _____   **Surface** _____

Temperature ____   **Humidity** ____   **Wind** ____   **Precipitation** _____

Training Grade for the Day

Physical status	A	B	C	D	F
Psychological status	A	B	C	D	F

Comments _____

_____

_____

Day 72

Thought for the Day

Don't Be Cruel

There's something majestic about building an Olympic stadium on a hilltop. It adds to the Olympian aura of the place. Barcelona called its setting a mountain. Trouble was, the marathoners had to climb this peak in the last couple of miles to reach their finish on the track. Atlanta's Olympic Stadium also sat on a hill. The rise was smaller than Barcelona's but still served as a final insult for runners who had come this far in the humid heat.

Whether by design or happenstance, both 1996 U.S. Trials also used courses with uphill finishes. The women qualified for their team in Columbia, South Carolina, and the men in Charlotte, North Carolina.

Cedric Jaggers wrote in the *Running Journal* that Columbia modified its Carolina Marathon course for the Women's Trials. But he reported that the would-be Olympians still faced "about a 200-foot climb during the last 10K." In Charlotte, the men ran "a new, more runner-friendly course." But the finish remained noticeably uphill.

"Uphill finishes are considered by most runners to be a form of cruel and unusual punishment," Jaggers wrote. "But it is better to be cruel and unusual in the Trials and eliminate those runners who are not as good uphill, since the Olympics would have a similar cruel finish."

That's one way of looking at it. Another is to recognize that marathons are punishing enough without adding cruel and unusual elements.

Tip for the Day

Build a minivacation around the marathon, if possible. Plan to arrive early to shake off travel fatigue—especially if the trip involves a time-zone change—and arrange to linger for a day or two after the race.

Day 72

Date _____

Plan _____

Training for the Day

Training Session

Type   Long ____   Fast ____   Easy ____   Other (specify) _____

Distance _____   **Time** _____

Pace _____   **Splits** _____ / _____ / _____ / _____ / _____

Effort   Max ____   Hard ____   Moderate ____   Mild ____   Rest ____

Warm-up _____   **Cool-down** _____

Cross-training (specify) _____

Training Conditions

Location _____   **Time of day** _____

People   Trained alone ____   Trained w/partner ____   Trained w/group ____

Terrain _____   **Surface** _____

Temperature ____   **Humidity** ____   **Wind** ____   **Precipitation** _____

Training Grade for the Day

Physical status   A   B   C   D   F

Psychological status   A   B   C   D   F

Comments _____

_____

_____

Day 73

Thought for the Day

Getting Over It

Early excitement had given way to doubt bordering on dread. Shannon had committed to running a marathon, started training, and picked a race. Then she learned the nature of her choice. She aired her concern in a letter to me from her home in North Carolina.

"I understand that the course is considered to be one of the more challenging on the East Coast," she wrote. "What advice can you offer a first-time marathoner on a hilly course?"

Despite what you might have read into previous Thoughts, I'm no hill hater. I don't limit myself to the courses advertised as "flat and fast." My history is dotted with marathons that cross mountain passes, like Ocean-to-Bay and Summit in northern California, and Deseret News in Utah. Before seeking them out, I had to adjust my attitude toward hills.

I first got to know them as a cross-country runner in the Midwest. We were taught to "work the hills," which I took to mean "fight your way over the top." This approach might have worked on the speed bumps that we called hills back there on the plains. But it didn't work on the imposing slopes, rising hundreds or thousands of feet, that I encountered out west. Those hills shrugged off my feeble attempts to fight them. The harder I worked, the sooner they humbled me.

A veteran mountain man, whose name I wish I'd remembered, turned my thinking around. "You're making the fundamental mistake that all rookies do on steep hills," he said.

Tip for the Day

Wear used shoes. They should have passed the test of your longest run. It's too late now to change shoes, because you couldn't adequately break in and test the new ones.

Day 73

Date _____

Plan _____

Training for the Day

Training Session

Type   Long ____   Fast ____   Easy ____   Other (specify) _____

Distance _____   **Time** _____

Pace _____   **Splits** _____ / _____ / _____ / _____ / _____

Effort   Max ____   Hard ____   Moderate ____   Mild ____   Rest ____

Warm-up _____   **Cool-down** _____

Cross-training (specify) _____

Training Conditions

Location _____   **Time of day** _____

People   Trained alone ____   Trained w/partner ____   Trained w/group ____

Terrain _____   **Surface** _____

Temperature ____   **Humidity** ____   **Wind** ____   **Precipitation** _____

Training Grade for the Day

Physical status   A   B   C   D   F

Psychological status   A   B   C   D   F

Comments _____

_____

_____

Day 74

Thought for the Day

Looking Up

"You can't fight these hills," the mountain man told me as I asked his advice on running up. "They always win if you do. You have to work *with* them, not against them."

And how did he suggest doing that? By *not* fighting to hold a steady pace, he said. You obviously have to work much harder on a hill than on the flat to run at the same pace, and the cost is too great. Instead, concentrate on holding the *effort* steady while going uphill. To use a driving or cycling term, shift down into a slower climbing gear on the ascent, then resume normal speed on the other side.

Mountain Man's advice let me make permanent peace with hills. If I treat them with respect, they let me pass through unbroken.

This was the gist of my answer to Shannon, the first-time marathoner: Don't fear or fight the hills; work with them. "Take care on downhills too," I added. "Don't let gravity carry you away, but instead hold yourself back to save your legs from taking an awful pounding. Keep the stride low, and let the slightly bent knees act as shock absorbers."

Practicing all these techniques on hilly training courses builds confidence along with leg strength. I advised Shannon to rehearse the marathon course's hills in her long runs.

Shannon wrote again after the marathon. Her excitement bubbled off the page: "I followed the advice about working with the hills. My confidence was great, and I knew that I would have a strong finish." She'd come a long way from the dread written all over her first letter. She wrote now, "The hills were my favorite part of the course."

Tip for the Day

Peek again at the course map. Memorize the locations of hills (both ups and downs), key mile points, and aid stations. Decide also where family and friends can see you along the route.

Day 74

Date _____

Plan _____

Training for the Day

Training Session

Type   Long ____   Fast ____   Easy ____   Other (specify) _____

Distance _____   **Time** _____

Pace _____   **Splits** _____ / _____ / _____ / _____ / _____

Effort   Max ____   Hard ____   Moderate ____   Mild ____   Rest ____

Warm-up _____   **Cool-down** _____

Cross-training (specify) _____

Training Conditions

Location _____   **Time of day** _____

People   Trained alone ____   Trained w/partner ____   Trained w/group ____

Terrain _____   **Surface** _____

Temperature ____   **Humidity** ____   **Wind** ____   **Precipitation** _____

Training Grade for the Day

Physical status   A   B   C   D   F

Psychological status   A   B   C   D   F

Comments _____

_____

_____

Day 75

Thought for the Day

Bridge Work

How do you describe paradise in a few hundred words? I could spend this whole chapter just raving about the setting of the Big Sur Marathon, which runs along one of the world's most gorgeous meetings of land and water.

Truth is, though, that spending most of an April morning passing between Big Sur and Carmel on the California coast left me with only vague recollections of how it all looked. Marathoners—even slow ones—don't absorb enough of any race's scenery at the time to recall many of its details later.

Only one clear picture from this course stays with me. It's the Bixby Creek Bridge. You know the bridge. Maybe you don't know its name or location, but you've seen it. Bixby has starred in dozens of magazine ads and TV commercials. Its arches span a deep, narrow canyon where the creek exits into the sea.

The local newspaper opened its results supplement with a huge color photo of Bixby in all its splendor. Runners flowed downhill toward the bridge. They had run through rain and hail early, then up a two-mile hill to the highest—and windiest—spot on the course. Hurricane Point had slapped their faces with 40-mile-an-hour gusts.

Now the sun was out and the wind had eased. The course would run generally downward from here to the finish. The runners in the picture might have thought the worst was past, but they would be wrong. No marathon gets easier later.

Tip for the Day

Check your entry. You should have mailed it months ago, but has it been confirmed? If not, place a call to the marathon office. Ask if your number will be mailed or if you pick it up on race weekend.

Day 75

Date _____

Plan _____

Training for the Day

Training Session

Type   Long ____   Fast ____   Easy ____   Other (specify) _____

Distance _____   **Time** _____

Pace _____   **Splits** _____ / _____ / _____ / _____ / _____

Effort   Max ____   Hard ____   Moderate ____   Mild ____   Rest ____

Warm-up _____   **Cool-down** _____

Cross-training (specify) _____

Training Conditions

Location _____   **Time of day** _____

People   Trained alone ____   Trained w/partner ____   Trained w/group ____

Terrain _____   **Surface** _____

Temperature ____   **Humidity** ____   **Wind** ____   **Precipitation** _____

Training Grade for the Day

Physical status	A	B	C	D	F
Psychological status	A	B	C	D	F

Comments _____

_____

_____

Day 76

Thought for the Day

The Harder Half

The halfway point only marks the end of the beginning in any marathon, and the Bixby Creek Bridge sits exactly 13 miles from either end of the Big Sur Marathon.

The bridge looks more dramatic in photos than it does from road level. You come upon it suddenly after rounding a corner, can't see its graceful arches from that angle, and don't notice the waves hitting the rocks hundreds of feet below unless you look quickly. This crossing takes only about a minute. But it still represented a turning point in my marathon, a bridge between the usual and the magical.

I've quit racing marathons. And for this one, my training had stopped at the half-marathon distance. So the Bixby Bridge represented a crossing from the normal into the abnormal, the known into the unknown. The real work started here, with half the distance still ahead.

I placed my faith in the magic of raceday—the three thousand runners, the heavenly course, the split shouters, the aid givers, the music players, the late-race cheerers—to carry me twice as far as usual. I wasn't sure that magic would be enough. You can never be sure. That's what makes the marathon so fearsome and so fascinating.

You must wait so long to answer the question, "Do I have what it takes to finish?" The deeper you go into the abnormal and unknown, the more you wonder. Then you finish. And you wonder later, How did I do that? Exactly what happened in that magical land on the far side of the bridge?

Tip for the Day

Make this your last week of normal training before the marathon. And even now, with the countdown at little more than two weeks, your distance is dropping. Limit your big days this week to semi-long and fast runs.

Day 76

Date _____

Plan _____

Training for the Day

Training Session

Type   Long ____   Fast ____   Easy ____   Other (specify) _____

Distance _____   **Time** _____

Pace _____ **Splits** _____ / _____ / _____ / _____ / _____

Effort   Max ____   Hard ____   Moderate ____   Mild ____   Rest ____

Warm-up _____   **Cool-down** _____

Cross-training (specify) _____

Training Conditions

Location _____   **Time of day** _____

People   Trained alone ____   Trained w/partner ____   Trained w/group ____

Terrain _____   **Surface** _____

Temperature ____   **Humidity** ____   **Wind** ____   **Precipitation** _____

Training Grade for the Day

Physical status   A   B   C   D   F

Psychological status   A   B   C   D   F

Comments _____

_____

_____

Day 77

Thought for the Day

Ever So Humble

If you want to know the runner you really are, not the one you once were or imagine yourself becoming, run a marathon. Any marathon will do.

One of my humblers happened to be Avenue of the Giants. It always cuts a runner down to size. The Avenue's course isn't hard, and its weather usually isn't harsh. Even on a rare warm day, giant redwoods shade 90 percent of the distance. Road signs warn drivers to use headlights all day.

The giant trees seem to shrink you. They've taken as long as two thousand years to grow as tall as 300 feet. The redwoods are room-sized at their base. They take so long to pass that you seem to run in slow motion. The forest swallows sounds, stilling runners' voices and quieting footfalls.

The Avenue was especially humbling when I ran it in an unusually hot year. I turned into one big cramp in the late miles and walked more often than planned. Pride had been set aside.

A woman and I hopscotched ahead of each other while trading walking breaks. She said, "I see you've become a biathlete too." I laughed. Later I traded good wishes with another fellow struggler. "Do whatever it takes to finish," I told him. He responded, "And keep doing it for however long it takes." All three of us finished. The redwoods didn't bow down to us. What we did was important only to us.

Marathoners can say of their finishes what pilots say of their landings. Any you can walk away from is good enough to let you take a small measure of pride along with the big dose of humility.

Tip for the Day

Stay extra alert to stress symptoms—a minor injury, the beginnings of a cold. Drop a scheduled run this week rather than risk an ailment that might stay with you through marathon day.

Day 77

Date _____

Plan _____

Training for the Day

Training Session

Type   Long ____   Fast ____   Easy ____   Other (specify) _____

Distance _____   **Time** _____

Pace _____   **Splits** _____ / _____ / _____ / _____ / _____

Effort   Max ____   Hard ____   Moderate ____   Mild ____   Rest ____

Warm-up _____   **Cool-down** _____

Cross-training (specify) _____

Training Conditions

Location _____   **Time of day** _____

People Trained alone ____   Trained w/partner ____   Trained w/group ____

Terrain _____   **Surface** _____

Temperature ____   **Humidity** ____   **Wind** ____   **Precipitation** _____

Training Grade for the Day

Physical status   A   B   C   D   F

Psychological status   A   B   C   D   F

Comments _____

_____

_____

The streets of New York City are friendly on marathon day. Some of the loudest cheers are reserved for the oldest runners.

WEEK TWELVE:
Tapering Off

Down comes your training to a final low-stress test of marathon pace and equipment. Run for one hour, at the pace and in the shoes and clothes you've selected for raceday. Otherwise you'll do little more than run easily and rest. As your training comes down, you can expect your energy and enthusiasm to rise and your nagging aches and pains to disappear. At the same time, however, it's normal to start imagining that you're coming down with a new illness or injury at the worst possible time. You probably aren't catching anything, but this is your mind's way of protecting you against training too much, too late. Choose your program below, assign workouts to the next seven days' diary pages, and add details there for completed training.

Cruiser Program
Big day: semi-long run of one hour, covering whatever distance feels comfortable in that time.
Other training days: three or four easy runs of 30 to 45 minutes each, with walking breaks optional.
Rest days: two or three with no running, but possibly cross-training.

Pacer Program
Big day: semi-long run of one hour at marathon pace.
Other training days: four to five easy runs of 30 to 60 minutes each.
Rest days: one or two with no running, but possibly cross-training.

Racer Program
Long day: semi-long run of one hour at marathon pace.
Fast day: one- to three-mile run at current 10K race pace (this may be broken into shorter intervals that total one to three miles, not counting recovery periods). Warm up and cool down with easy running.
Other training days: four easy runs of 30 to 60 minutes each.
Rest days: one with no running, but possibly cross-training.

Day 78

Thought for the Day

How They Taper

The hard part of training isn't the work. It's knowing what *not* to do, and why, and for how long—then heeding those limits.

Top runners are trained to do more and faster. They do this well. What they do reluctantly is quit working in the final days before a big event. Tapering goes against the nature of people accustomed to running twice a day and collecting triple-figure mileage.

Yet training down before a race is exactly what they need. It's what we all need, but their cutbacks are more dramatic than ours and their temptation is greater to squeeze in one last hard workout, one day too late.

While surveying athletes for an earlier book, I asked 80 runners how they taper. Gary Fanelli, once a 2:14 marathoner, voiced the mixed feelings of this group. "Tapering can be tricky," said Fanelli. "Too much rest, and one feels sluggish. Not enough, and one feels tired."

Just as these runners train by similar patterns, they follow the same general guidelines for tapering. The details obviously differ with the distance and importance of the race, and with the age of the runner.

Gabriele Andersen, of 1984 Olympic collapse fame, confessed to taking "not much" taper back then. "Now I know better," she said. "Twelve years later—and older, at 50—I taper more."

John Treacy, an Olympic Marathon medalist in 1984, also respects the aging process. "At this stage in my career," he wrote at age 38, "the body needs more time to recover."

Tip for the Day

Don't fret too much about your marathon prospects. If you have trained properly, if the long runs have reached planned length, and if you've stayed healthy, it's all but guaranteed to go well.

Day 78

Date _____

Plan _____

Training for the Day

Training Session

Type   Long ____   Fast ____   Easy ____   Other (specify) _____

Distance _____   **Time** _____

Pace _____   **Splits** _____ / _____ / _____ / _____ / _____

Effort   Max ____   Hard ____   Moderate ____   Mild ____   Rest ____

Warm-up _____   **Cool-down** _____

Cross-training (specify) _____

Training Conditions

Location _____   **Time of day** _____

People   Trained alone ____   Trained w/partner ____   Trained w/group ____

Terrain _____   **Surface** _____

Temperature ____   **Humidity** ____   **Wind** ____   **Precipitation** _____

Training Grade for the Day

Physical status   A   B   C   D   F

Psychological status   A   B   C   D   F

Comments _____

_____

_____

Day 79

Thought for the Day

Tapering Tactics

Several general patterns of tapering cover most of the top runners I questioned for the book *Road Racers & Their Training*:

- One to three weeks of gradually decreasing mileage
- Last long run at least two weeks before the race
- Last hard workout a week or more before
- Something fast in the last few days
- Final one to three days very easy or off

Mileage typically drops by as much as half. Olympic champion Frank Shorter said, "I ran the same sequence [of workouts as usual], but cut the amount in half" during his final taper. Julie Isphording, a 1984 Olympian, used a last-week mileage countdown of 8-7-6-5-4-3-race.

Half-distance training often applies as well to the long run a week before the race. Ultrarunner Ann Trason goes "no more than 20 miles" then, although she's accustomed to weekend 30 to 50 milers. Dan Held, a 2:13 marathoner, routinely runs 20 to 25 miles, but "I don't run longer than 13 miles the week prior."

Workouts taper off in intensity as well as speed. Amby Burfoot, a Boston Marathon winner, runs "a little less but a lot easier."

Everyone eases down near zero on race eve. A common pattern is to rest two days before the race, then run lightly the last day.

Ingrid Kristiansen, who has held the women's marathon record for more than 11 years, wrote that rest is best at the end of the taper: "Be confident that you don't lose anything from taking some days totally off, but you actually gain a lot."

Tip for the Day

Consider what causes bad marathons. Mostly it's running too few or too many miles in training. Another common source of problems occurs in the tapering period: running too much, too late.

Day 79

Date _____

Plan _____

Training for the Day

Training Session

Type　　Long ____　Fast ____　Easy ____　Other (specify) _____

Distance _____　**Time** _____

Pace _____　**Splits** _____ / _____ / _____ / _____ / _____

Effort　　Max ____　Hard ____　Moderate ____　Mild ____　Rest ____

Warm-up _____　**Cool-down** _____

Cross-training (specify) _____

Training Conditions

Location _____　**Time of day** _____

People　Trained alone ____　Trained w/partner ____　Trained w/group ____

Terrain _____　**Surface** _____

Temperature ____　**Humidity** ____　**Wind** ____　**Precipitation** _____

Training Grade for the Day

Physical status	A	B	C	D	F
Psychological status	A	B	C	D	F

Comments _____

_____

_____

Day 80

Thought for the Day

The Taper Paper

For too long, runners and running researchers didn't speak the same language. We runners didn't hear or couldn't understand much of what the guys in white coats were learning.

Owen Anderson is changing all that. No one now writing about running does better at translating technical data from the labs into practical tips for the road than Anderson. The exercise scientist publishes the newsletter *Running Research News* and writes a column for *Runner's World*.

Scientists are professional skeptics. Even our most time-honored practices don't escape their scrutiny. Consider the traditional practices of premarathon tapering and postrace recovery. Anderson dissects them in an article titled "Are You Already 'Damaged Goods' When You Show Up for Your Races?"

He says that most runners take their last long run too close to the event and resume hard running too soon afterward. He quotes research papers as proof that the traditional two-week taper before a marathon and easy month after the race aren't enough.

The recovery study that Anderson cites isn't new but didn't reach many runners when it appeared in a 1985 issue of the *American Journal of Pathology*. Anderson unearthed the findings of Michael J. Warhol's team from Harvard and Tufts Universities, which tested 40 marathoners at various intervals after races. The damage of the race didn't begin to clear for about a month. This should give you some clue how the longest training run might affect you.

Tip for the Day

Don't try to pack in extra work the last week or two. It won't help. Nothing you do in training now will make your marathon better. But it's not too late to make it worse. It's never too late to hurt yourself.

Day 80

Date _____

Plan _____

Training for the Day

Training Session

Type   Long _____   Fast _____   Easy _____   Other (specify) _____

Distance _____   **Time** _____

Pace _____   **Splits** _____ / _____ / _____ / _____ / _____

Effort   Max _____   Hard _____   Moderate _____   Mild _____   Rest _____

Warm-up _____   **Cool-down** _____

Cross-training (specify) _____

Training Conditions

Location _____   **Time of day** _____

People   Trained alone _____   Trained w/partner _____   Trained w/group _____

Terrain _____   **Surface** _____

Temperature _____   **Humidity** _____   **Wind** _____   **Precipitation** _____

Training Grade for the Day

Physical status   A   B   C   D   F

Psychological status   A   B   C   D   F

Comments _____

_____ _____

_____

Day 81

Thought for the Day

Easy End of Training

Owen Anderson, editor of *Running Research News*, urges runners to rethink their spacing of the last long run and the race. He refers to a study by Dutch researcher Harm Kuipers and colleagues, reported by the *International Journal of Sports Medicine* in 1989. Their 23 runners trained and raced at three levels: for a 15K race, a 25K, and a marathon.

Kuipers found no muscle problems before the 15K race. Eight runners took these problems into the 25K, and 13 started the marathon with muscles already damaged. The damage is clearly distance related. It was present in marathoners, says Anderson, "in spite of the fact that the runners had completed a traditional [one-week] taper just before the marathon, which had included only 12 miles during the last week before the race."

Anderson's advice on tapering? Even more of it than I recommend: "One *month* of reduced training before a marathon is a pretty reasonable figure," he says.

How much to taper? Anderson echoes Kuipers's finding that "15K runs produced muscle damage in only a small minority of runners, so eight- to nine-mile runs can serve as your longest runs during this one-month period."

If marathoners need this much taper, why do they allow so little? "Runners are traditionalists," says Anderson. "They tend to do things the way they've always been done."

Runners also are pragmatists who'll adopt whatever works. Give us convincing new information and we'll start a new tradition.

Tip for the Day

Realize that training has a delayed-reaction effect. You don't draw your ability to run a marathon from what you run this week, but from a reservoir of fitness filled weeks and months earlier.

Day 81

Date _____

Plan _____

Training for the Day

Training Session

Type   Long ____   Fast ____   Easy ____   Other (specify) _____

Distance _____   **Time** _____

Pace _____   **Splits** _____ / _____ / _____ / _____ / _____

Effort   Max ____   Hard ____   Moderate ____   Mild ____   Rest ____

Warm-up _____   **Cool-down** _____

Cross-training (specify) _____

Training Conditions

Location _____   **Time of day** _____

People   Trained alone ____   Trained w/partner ____   Trained w/group ____

Terrain _____   **Surface** _____

Temperature ____   **Humidity** ____   **Wind** ____   **Precipitation** _____

Training Grade for the Day

Physical status	A	B	C	D	F
Psychological status	A	B	C	D	F

Comments _____

_____

_____

Day 82

Thought for the Day

Flex Time

Runners want anchors. We want to cling to clear, definitive rules. We want programs to follow, quotas to meet, measures of certainty in an uncertain world. Schedules tell us what to do, which can be comforting. But a prearranged schedule that doesn't adjust to immediate feelings can be damaging—especially in the last weeks before a marathon.

Somewhat unsettling advice, which asks us to let go of our anchors, pops up in my writing. A pair of Scandinavians, multirecord setter Ingrid Kristiansen and four-time Olympic winner Lasse Viren, endorse this approach of running by feel, not by plan.

Kristiansen refused my request for her training schedule, claiming it would mislead readers. She spoke only in generalities. "My body always knows best how a workout should be done, and it will tell me if I am willing to listen," she said. "This is something most people in the Western world have forgotten. African athletes use their intuition. If they are tired, they rest and have no guilt feelings about it."

I didn't try to draw any training details from Viren. He covered the subject with the same broad strokes as Kristiansen. "Hard training is given too much importance nowadays. Training is most effective when it feels relaxed," Viren said. "Basic training is not meant to feel like torture. I'm afraid runners train too hard today. They would rather believe their computers than their feelings."

Tip for the Day

Go into the race well rested by allowing at least two weeks of gradually dwindling effort. Extrahard work in these final days does nothing but drain your energy pool at the worst possible time.

Day 82

Date _____

Plan _____

Training for the Day

Training Session

Type Long ____ Fast ____ Easy ____ Other (specify) _____

Distance _____ **Time** _____

Pace _____ **Splits** _____ / _____ / _____ / _____ /

Effort Max ____ Hard ____ Moderate ____ Mild ____ Rest ____

Warm-up _____ **Cool-down** _____

Cross-training (specify) _____

Training Conditions

Location _____ **Time of day** _____

People Trained alone ____ Trained w/partner ____ Trained w/group ____

Terrain _____ **Surface** _____

Temperature ____ **Humidity** ____ **Wind** ____ **Precipitation** _____

Training Grade for the Day

Physical status   A   B   C   D   F

Psychological status   A   B   C   D   F

Comments _____

_____

_____

Day 83

Thought for the Day

Flexibility Exercise

Runners who are trying to break computer-like training habits still want guidelines. They don't want to cast themselves completely adrift, but want to hold onto a flexible plan. As someone trying to break the grip of rigid programs, I've come up with a plan that combines the need for a goal with the greater need for flexibility:

- Start each run only intending to see how far my legs want to go. A warm-up mile or so will tell me.

- Run as much or as little as the day will allow (and as fast or slowly as the day dictates). It might only be that warm-up mile, but it also could be an hour or more.

- Take as many days as needed to complete one to two hours. Then take a day off.

This plan gives a reasonable goal while letting day-to-day and mile-to-mile feelings decide what to do. It lets me run more days than not. It mixes longer and shorter runs, faster and slower ones, work and rest in satisfying amounts.

Lasse Viren and Ingrid Kristiansen might approve. "When I feel like running fast, I run fast," said Viren. "When I feel tired, I take it easy." Kristiansen added that training "consists of two phases—the work phase and the rest phase. Both have the same importance, and the balance of the two gives the final result of the workout"—and the entire program.

Tip for the Day

Run minimum amounts in the last week or two before the marathon, and plan to rest completely the final day or two. Save the trained-in strength for the biggest day, when you need it most.

Day 83

Date _____

Plan _____

Training for the Day

Training Session

Type   Long _____   Fast _____   Easy _____   Other (specify) _____

Distance _____   **Time** _____

Pace _____   **Splits** _____ / _____ / _____ / _____ / _____

Effort   Max _____   Hard _____   Moderate _____   Mild _____   Rest _____

Warm-up _____   **Cool-down** _____

Cross-training (specify) ___   _____

Training Conditions

Location _____   **Time of day** _____

People   Trained alone ___   Trained w/partner ___   Trained w/group ___

Terrain _____   **Surface** _____

Temperature _____   **Humidity** _____   **Wind** _____   **Precipitation** _____

Training Grade for the Day

Physical status	A	B	C	D	F
Psychological status	A	B	C	D	F

Comments _____

_____

_____

Day 84

Thought for the Day

Take Care

It had been a routine trip. My son dozed beside me as I drove down the freeway in the flow of traffic. I was taking him to his mom's before leaving for my Honolulu Marathon.

Suddenly we felt and heard a "whomp!" A speeder had rear-ended our little Honda, which fishtailed out of control and onto the muddy shoulder, where it rolled. Eric and I looked like crash-test dummies, hanging from what was now the car's roof. We weren't injured, thanks to seat belts.

Everything loose in the car was ejected except us. The car was a total loss, but we weren't the slightest bit bruised or scratched. I didn't even miss the vacation and marathon I'd planned for that week.

At the risk of sounding like one of those cheaply made public-service ads you see on TV, please buckle your belts whenever you climb into a car. They work. I ran my marathon as scheduled that weekend.

As long as I'm being preachy, let me urge you to take care of yourself in other ways where running itself offers little or no protection. You may need professional help in the form of regular medical exams for a variety of conditions—from breast cancer in women to prostate cancer in men to heart disease for all. Routine checkups have extended the active lives of many of my runner friends.

Running itself can't always keep you going. Sometimes you need help from modern doctors, or from modern safety devices such as seat belts. Promise yourself and your family and friends to use them so you can stay in the running.

Tip for the Day

Expect any of your physical ailments to magnify as the marathon approaches. Imaginary problems become real and small ones grow large. Also expect them to do no real damage and to vanish when the race begins.

Day 84

Date _____

Plan _____

Training for the Day

Training Session

Type Long _____ Fast _____ Easy _____ Other (specify) _____

Distance _____ **Time** _____

Pace _____ **Splits** _____ / _____ / _____ / _____ / _____

Effort Max _____ Hard _____ Moderate _____ Mild _____ Rest _____

Warm-up _____ **Cool-down** _____

Cross-training (specify) _____

Training Conditions

Location _____ **Time of day** _____

People Trained alone _____ Trained w/partner _____ Trained w/group _____

Terrain _____ **Surface** _____

Temperature _____ **Humidity** _____ **Wind** _____ **Precipitation** _____

Training Grade for the Day

Physical status   A   B   C   D   F

Psychological status   A   B   C   D   F

Comments _____

_____

_____

Francie Larrieu Smith (No. 2) is one of America's most durable athletes, making Olympic teams from 1972 to 1992.

WEEK THIRTEEN:
Resting Up

Nothing you do this week can train you any better for the marathon. It's too late for that. However, it's never too late to undermine your race by trying to cram in last-minute work. Don't stop running completely in this final week, which could throw you too far off your routine. But limit yourself to easy runs (even easier than during a normal week), while taking an extra day or two of rest. This also could be your travel week. Arrive in the marathon city soon enough, deal with any jet lag, preview the course, pick up your race packet, and spend some time sampling the excitement that a marathon weekend has to offer. Choose your program below, assign workouts to the next seven days' diary pages, and add details there for completed training.

Cruiser Program
Big day: none.
Other training days: three or four easy runs of about 30 minutes each, with walking breaks optional.
Rest days: three or four with no running, but possibly cross-training early in the week.

Pacer Program
Big day: none.
Other training days: four to five easy runs of about 30 minutes each.
Rest days: two or three with no running, but possibly cross-training early in the week.

Racer Program
Long day: none.
Fast day: none, but possibly some light speedwork in easy runs.
Other training days: four to six easy runs of about 30 minutes each.
Rest days: one to three with no running, but possibly cross-training early in the week.

Day 85

Thought for the Day

It Never Fails

Marie from Seattle called to report on her marathon the past weekend. I'd advised her a little during training and asked her to check in afterward. "The training went well until my last long run," she said. "I did OK in it too, but came down with shin splints right after that."

She complained of not being able to train enough in the last three weeks. I asked if the injury had affected her marathon. "Not at all," she told me. "I was amazed that the problem vanished."

I'm not surprised. This type of premarathon injury, less serious than it seems, happens all the time and for good reasons. I know the syndrome well.

I write this while tapering for a marathon. The words will go down haltingly, because I'll stop every few sentences to examine an injury or illness. Both Achilles tendons hurt, as do my left knee and right calf. My throat and tummy ache. This week, I'm keeping my distance from journalism-school students who look as if they could pass on a cold or flu. I'm ducking household chores that might tweak a muscle or inflame a tendon.

Something always goes wrong in these final days. If the ailment isn't real, I dream one up while passing every twinge and tickle under a mental microscope.

The examples of medical crises and miracles abound. It's as much a part of the marathon experience as running those miles.

Tip for the Day

Find out what the on-course drinks will be and where they'll be available. If they are the wrong type or there aren't enough of them, make private plans for special delivery of your liquids.

Day 85

Date _____

Plan _____

Training for the Day

Training Session

Type   Long ____   Fast ____   Easy ____   Other (specify) _____

Distance _____   **Time** _____

Pace _____   **Splits** _____ / _____ / _____ / _____ / _____

Effort   Max ____   Hard ____   Moderate ____   Mild ____   Rest ____

Warm-up _____   **Cool-down** _____

Cross-training (specify) _____

Training Conditions

Location _____   **Time of day** _____

People   Trained alone ____   Trained w/partner ____   Trained w/group ____

Terrain _____   **Surface** _____

Temperature ____   **Humidity** ____   **Wind** ____   **Precipitation** _____

Training Grade for the Day

Physical status   A   B   C   D   F

Psychological status   A   B   C   D   F

Comments _____

_____

_____

Day 86

Thought for the Day

Imaginary Injuries

It never fails. I can't recall going into any marathon healthy—or coming out of one uncured.

A knee had locked up during late runs before the Long Beach Marathon. The pain vanished in the first hour of the race. An intestinal bug struck before Avenue of the Giants. Abdominal cramps started the marathon with me, but they dropped out early. An auto wreck began Honolulu Marathon week. Sore and shaken, I still ran—and finished with a PW, but couldn't lay any of the blame on the accident's aftereffects.

A heavy round of yard work strained some butt muscles before Portland. Any butt dragging there resulted from fatigue, not injury. A sudden case of sciatica appeared two days before the Drake Relays Marathon, and a three-mile run that day sent fire down the backs of my legs. These symptoms just as suddenly disappeared on raceday. A calf muscle, torn in the last long run, threatened my Napa Valley race. I had several weeks to fear that it wouldn't heal well enough, soon enough. But of course it did.

Then came Achilles-tendon injuries (plural). These worried me, as well they should have with the Royal Victoria Marathon just days away. I couldn't see their value right then but would recognize it later.

I'd know then that the premarathon paranoia was normal, necessary, and even healthy. Later I'd see that it kept me from doing any foolish running too late. Then I'd marvel again at the healing powers of the marathon. It never fails.

Tip for the Day

Plan your last meal—what and when? Order the same foods you have eaten trouble-free before your long runs. Allow the same amount of time between that meal and the marathon as you did when training long.

Day 86

Date _____

Plan _____

Training for the Day

Training Session

Type   Long ____   Fast ____   Easy ____   Other (specify) _____

Distance _____   **Time** _____

Pace _____   **Splits** _____/ _____/ _____/ _____/ _____

Effort   Max ____   Hard ____   Moderate ____   Mild ____   Rest ____

Warm-up _____   **Cool-down** _____

Cross-training (specify) _____

Training Conditions

Location _____   **Time of day** _____

People   Trained alone ____   Trained w/partner ____   Trained w/group ____

Terrain _____   **Surface** _____

Temperature ____   **Humidity** ____   **Wind** ____   **Precipitation** _____

Training Grade for the Day

Physical status	A	B	C	D	F
Psychological status	A	B	C	D	F

Comments _____

_____

_____

Day 87

Thought for the Day

Psyching Down

After-dinner talks the night before marathons are my least favorite. I compete with the pasta and with adrenaline-fueled runners who'd rather talk with each other than listen to me. My talk in Fort McMurray, Alberta, was billed as "motivational." This contrasted with the instructional program, my favorite type, which had played to a less distracted audience that afternoon.

I opened the dinner show by saying, "My job here is to make sure you get a good night's sleep. I won't intentionally bore you into slumber, though that might happen too. My job is to help you relax, to psych you *down*."

Psyching up wasn't a problem for these runners. Their psyching had started months earlier when they marked this race on the calendar and started training for it. Each long run psyched them up more. Now they stared the marathon in the face. Emotions multiplied in this crowd, threatening to psych them *out*.

"I have just three things to tell you tonight," I said to any runner who happened to listen. "All are meant to calm you down."

Those three points:

1. The hardest part is over.
2. The fun starts now.
3. The race is a victory lap.

"Ninety-eight percent of winning," a sport psychologist friend of mine likes to remind fretful athletes, "is getting to the starting line." They're there.

Tip for the Day

Unless you intend to race at a five- to six-minute mile pace, forget about doing any warm-up running. Save every step for the marathon, and warm up over the first few miles as you settle into your pace.

Day 87

Date _____

Plan _____

Training for the Day

Training Session

Type   Long ____   Fast ____   Easy ____   Other (specify) _____

Distance _____   **Time** _____

Pace _____   **Splits** _____ / _____ / _____ / _____ / _____

Effort   Max ____   Hard ____   Moderate ____   Mild ____   Rest ____

Warm-up _____   **Cool-down** _____

Cross-training (specify) _____

Training Conditions

Location _____   **Time of day** _____

People   Trained alone ____   Trained w/partner ____   Trained w/group ____

Terrain _____   **Surface** _____

Temperature ____   **Humidity** ____   **Wind** ____   **Precipitation** _____

Training Grade for the Day

Physical status   A   B   C   D   F

Psychological status   A   B   C   D   F

Comments _____

_____

_____

Day 88

Thought for the Day

Your Victory Lap

"You did most of your training alone," I reminded the marathoners the night before the Fort McMurray Marathon. "You faced down the forces of injury, illness, and indifference—and now you're here at the starting line."

Now the fun could begin. Anyone who'd trained alone would delight in having company on the road in these final miles, and having splits, drinks, and cheers handed out from the roadside. Anyone who had come this far was all but guaranteed of finishing. About 98 percent of well-trained marathoners finish, and the other 2 percent probably start with conditions that should have kept them off the line.

"Finishing Is Winning," read the banner behind me in the Fort McMurray dining room. In the two previous runnings of this marathon, no one had failed to win.

Anyone who even starts a marathon has already won in one sense. The race is the victory lap. He or she has already left behind the 9 in 10 people who never run at all, the 9 in 10 runners who never enter races, and the 9 in 10 racers who never try marathons.

"A marathon is never easy," I said to this group. "But you wouldn't want it to be."

The movie *A League of Their Own* deals with baseball but has a scene that speaks directly to marathoners. The Geena Davis character complains about the difficulties of her sport. "Hard?" replies Tom Hanks's character. "It is supposed to be hard. If it wasn't hard, everybody would do it. Hard is what makes it good."

Tip for the Day

Start with the intention of making the first (warm-up) mile your slowest of the day. You probably have no choice while fighting the crowd, but don't let the early slowness trouble you. You'll soon be up to speed.

Day 88

Date _____

Plan _____

Training for the Day

Training Session

Type   Long ____   Fast ____   Easy ____   Other (specify) _____

Distance _____   **Time** _____

Pace _____   **Splits** _____ / _____ / _____ / _____ / _____

Effort   Max ____   Hard ____   Moderate ____   Mild ____   Rest ____

Warm-up _____   **Cool-down** _____

Cross-training (specify) _____

Training Conditions

Location _____   **Time of day** _____

People   Trained alone ____   Trained w/partner ____   Trained w/group ____

Terrain _____   **Surface** _____

Temperature ____   **Humidity** ____   **Wind** ____   **Precipitation** _____

Training Grade for the Day

Physical status   A   B   C   D   F

Psychological status   A   B   C   D   F

Comments _____

_____

_____

Day 89

Thought for the Day

Winning Is . . .

George Sheehan, running's best-loved writer and speaker, who died in 1993, is still getting plenty of mileage from his written and spoken lines. Somewhere he must be smiling, knowing he has won in the best possible way that a communicator can.

I titled his biography *Did I Win?* People who haven't read past its cover ask, "What does that title mean?" Those who haven't reached the last chapter wonder, "Well, did he win?"

George supplied that title himself. "I was standing at the altar of a Unitarian Church, answering questions from the runners in front of me," he recalled in a column sparked by one of his last talks. The depth of the questions surprised him. They didn't deal with how to run a faster marathon or how to treat tendinitis. The question that led to the column was what his big concern was at this stage of life.

"I was silent for a moment," he wrote. "Then with my arms in front of me, palms upward as if in supplication, I looked heavenward and asked, 'Did I win?'" George was still asking himself if he'd been a good enough writer, speaker, runner, doctor, father, husband, friend. Had he done enough?

The *Did I Win?* book tallies up his victories. There were also losses, of course, because no one goes through life undefeated. But George surely lived his 75 years with a winning record.

A tribute dinner honored him in April 1993. The five hundred guests each received a photo of him running, and below it one of his favorite lines. It read, "Winning is never having to say I quit." Nowhere is that more true than in a marathon, where you win simply by not quitting on yourself.

Tip for the Day

Time yourself. Click on your watch only as you cross the starting line (not when the gun sounds). This way, you insure yourself of more accurate splits and final time than the "official" clocks show.

Day 89

Date _____

Plan _____

Training for the Day

Training Session

Type   Long ____   Fast ____   Easy ____   Other (specify) _____

Distance _____   **Time** _____

Pace _____ **Splits** _____ / _____ / _____ / _____ / _____

Effort   Max ____   Hard ____   Moderate ____   Mild ____   Rest ____

Warm-up _____   **Cool-down** _____

Cross-training (specify) _____

Training Conditions

Location _____   **Time of day** _____

People   Trained alone ____   Trained w/partner ____   Trained w/group ____

Terrain _____   **Surface** _____

Temperature ____   **Humidity** ____   **Wind** ____   **Precipitation** _____

Training Grade for the Day

Physical status   A   B   C   D   F

Psychological status   A   B   C   D   F

Comments _____

_____

_____

Day 90

Thought for the Day

Tears and Cheers

The finish line of a long race is its emotional center. Standing there, you see and hear runners laugh, cry, shout, and groan from effort, pain, relief, joy.

The Capital City Festival in Edmonton, Alberta, was an emotional first for Laura Weir. Two years earlier, when she was 19, Laura had crashed while driving on a mountain road. The accident left her with head injuries so severe that doctors first doubted her survival.

She survived. Then the doctors doubted she would ever come out of her coma. "That told us the chances of any sort of recovery were not positive," says her father, Mike Weir.

After six weeks, Laura woke up, but doctors doubted she would walk again. She stayed in the hospital for almost a year, progressing from a wheelchair to assisted walking to moving on her own.

Laura set as her goal the Edmonton marathon. "I told myself I had no excuse," she says. "After having been active, I wanted to do something again. Running was the one thing I could do."

Her vision, balance, and speech are all affected by the brainstem injury. She can't tie her shoes, she shakes hands with difficulty, and her words come slowly and softly.

She trained well for the marathon, both accommodating and challenging her limits. Running the open roads alone is risky for her, so she trained on either a short street loop or a track—often an *indoor* track. That meant running the short laps for hours at a time.

Come raceday, Laura showed little emotion and shed no apparent tears as she finished in 4:39. She'd met bigger challenges than this. But she dampened the eyes of spectators who knew her story.

Tip for the Day

Divide your marathon into two equal parts. Feel that you're holding back in the first half when your natural urge is to speed up.

Day 90

Date _____

Plan _____

Training for the Day

Training Session

Type   Long ____   Fast ____   Easy ____   Other (specify) _____

Distance _____   **Time** _____

Pace _____   **Splits** _____ / _____ / _____ / _____ / _____

Effort   Max ____   Hard ____   Moderate ____   Mild ____   Rest ____

Warm-up _____   **Cool-down** _____

Cross-training (specify) _____

Training Conditions

Location _____   **Time of day** _____

People   Trained alone ____   Trained w/partner ____   Trained w/group ____

Terrain _____   **Surface** _____

Temperature ____   **Humidity** ____   **Wind** ____   **Precipitation** _____

Training Grade for the Day

Physical status   A   B   C   D   F

Psychological status   A   B   C   D   F

Comments _____

_____

_____

Day 91

Thought for the Day

This Run's for You

Running a marathon can be—*should* be—a team sport. As you prepare to run yours, think of someone who helped bring you this far and will help carry you the rest of the way. Some thoughts from marathoners on their special forms of teamwork:

- Tim Brown of Parlin, New Jersey: After deciding to enter the New York City Marathon, I lost my Aunt Helen to cancer. My parents had both died before I was three, and Aunt Helen had filled in the blanks with stories about the mom and dad I never knew. I dedicated the run to her, and we had a great chat for almost five hours. Whenever I started to doubt myself, Aunt Helen made me continue. Do angels wear running shoes?

- Jesse Diaz of Granite City, Illinois: While I prepared for a marathon in November, my wife, Norma, was pregnant. She kept saying do this for "your daughters." (We had only one girl at the time, but I think Norma knew she was carrying another daughter.) Crystal was born in September. Throughout the race, Crystal's image was clear in my mind. The result was a PR by 20 minutes. I finished with tears of happiness.

- Maria Cobb of Anchorage, Alaska: There's a "who" behind everyone who enters a marathon. And, I might add, there's a "who" behind everyone who breathes! When we acknowledge that—if only in our hearts—we give credit and meaning to that person. We should not ever underestimate the power of this acknowledgment to either ourselves or that person.

Tip for the Day

Run the second half of your marathon much differently than the first. Push on when your natural urge is to slow down. Take pleasure in passing the people who passed you earlier.

Day 91

Date _____

Plan _____

Training for the Day

Training Session

Type   Long ____   Fast ____   Easy ____   Other (specify) _____

Distance _____   **Time** _____

Pace _____   **Splits** _____ / _____ / _____ / _____ / _____

Effort   Max ____   Hard ____   Moderate ____   Mild ____   Rest ____

Warm-up _____   **Cool-down** _____

Cross-training (specify) _____

Training Conditions

Location _____   **Time of day** _____

People   Trained alone ____   Trained w/partner ____   Trained w/group ____

Terrain _____   **Surface** _____

Temperature ____   **Humidity** ____   **Wind** ____   **Precipitation** _____

Training Grade for the Day

Physical status   A   B   C   D   F

Psychological status   A   B   C   D   F

Comments _____

_____

_____

New York City's finish-line clock tells a success story: This flock of marathoners has broken the 3-1/2 hour barrier.

WEEK FOURTEEN:
Doing It

It's here at last. Three months after you entered this program, you reach its graduation day. This is the culmination of all that you've planned, worked for, worried about. This weekend, you become a marathoner for the first time, or you rewrite your personal record, or you climb higher on the list of finishers, or you add to your count of finishes.

Unlike all other chapters in the book, this one covers only two days. The first is marathon day. You know all about what needs to be done then. But you might not have thought much about the next day, which is just as important—if somewhat less exciting. This is when you travel home and take bows for your marathon result, when you savor all that you've done, when you nurse your sore muscles, and most of all when you start recovering. The quickest and best way to recover is by avoiding the activity that caused the damage. Don't try to run out the soreness; rest it. Eat more than usual, drink more, brag more, sit more, sleep more. But don't run at all the day after your marathon. In fact, hold off doing any further running until the pain and stiffness ease. Choose your program below, assign workouts to the next two days' diary pages, and add details there for completed work.

Cruiser Program
Big day: cruise the marathon, running at the pace you've projected and taking walking breaks as you've practiced them.
Rest day: no running on the day after the marathon.

Pacer Program
Big day: pace the marathon, running at the tempo you've projected and keeping walking breaks as an option.
Rest day: no running on the day after the marathon.

Racer Program
Big day: race the marathon at the pace you've projected.
Rest day: no running on the day after the marathon.

Day 92

Thought for the Day

Happy Endings

Bob Scott thought he was tougher than this. Says the Los Angeles radio newsman, "I'm like a lot of journalists who cover hard news—more than a little cynical about life and people."

So here was Scott, standing near the end of the Los Angeles Marathon, crying shamelessly as the late-finishing runners passed by. Why? Because these were the last of the first-time marathoners he'd helped bring this far.

Scott's radio station, KNX, cosponsored a training group called the L.A. Leggers. For six months before the marathon, the Leggers met each Saturday for a long run and pep talk. They followed Jeff Galloway's training plan. "Jeff's *Book of Running* outlines perhaps the easiest way to prepare for a marathon," says Scott. "But make no mistake, these runners are involved in a vigorous training program."

Scott himself had used the plan successfully. Now he passed it along as coordinator-cheerleader of the Leggers. Scott expected success from the program. What he hadn't counted on was the feeling of team spirit that grew among the Leggers and their leaders.

"It never entered my mind that I would become emotionally attached to these folks," he says. "But as we moved into the final weeks, I began to realize—as the runners probably had long before—that what I'd envisioned as a simple marathon-training program had become a community, almost a family."

Tip for the Day

Treat the marathon as your graduation exercise. In those few hours, celebrate the good work that made this day possible. It's your reward for all the effort put in over the last few months.

Day 92

Date _____

Plan _____

Training for the Day

Training Session

Type　Long ____　Fast ____　Easy ____　Other (specify) _____

Distance _____　**Time** _____

Pace _____　**Splits** _____ / _____ / _____ / _____ / _____

Effort　Max ____　Hard ____　Moderate ____　Mild ____　Rest ____

Warm-up _____　**Cool-down** _____

Cross-training (specify) _____

Training Conditions

Location _____　**Time of day** _____

People　Trained alone ____　Trained w/partner ____　Trained w/group ____

Terrain _____　**Surface** _____

Temperature ____　**Humidity** ____　**Wind** ____　**Precipitation** _____

Training Grade for the Day

Physical status　　　　　A　　B　　C　　D　　F

Psychological status　　A　　B　　C　　D　　F

Comments _____

_____

_____

Day 93

Thought for the Day

Sticking Together

The L.A. Leggers "family" sent 249 members to the starting line of the Los Angeles Marathon. All but one completed it.

Program coordinator Bob Scott says, "Our only nonfinisher knew he was a question mark from the start. He had developed a knee problem during our 24-mile run and was never able to recover. He made it to 15 miles [on raceday], and then the pain kicked in. I'd like to believe he remembered our advice about not flirting with more serious injury and pulled out."

Scott tells about two runners named Lloyd and Charlie. They ran their marathon together, and it didn't go as smoothly as they'd hoped. Charlie hit the wall at 23 miles and told his friend to go on without him. Lloyd refused, so they walked in together.

"Though I'm not a macho-type guy," says Scott, "I have a hard time letting anyone see me cry. But as I stood worrying about these last two of our folks on the course and they came around the last turn, the tears came and I didn't care."

Later the Leggers met for a victory party. The question most asked of Scott was, "What are we going to do now? You can't just let us go." He says, "There were no plans to continue the program through the spring. But we decided to meet on an informal basis once a month until we started weekly runs again in late July." One-third of these marathoners returned for the first monthly run without another marathon yet in sight.

Tip for the Day

Start your postrace celebration—along with your recovery—by eating soon after finishing. Carbohydrates fueled all those miles, and carbo reloading after a marathon helps you even more than loading up in advance.

Day 93

Date _____

Plan _____

Training for the Day

Training Session

Type   Long ____   Fast ____   Easy ____   Other (specify) _____

Distance _____   **Time** _____

Pace _____   **Splits** _____ / _____ / _____ / _____ / _____

Effort   Max ____   Hard ____   Moderate ____   Mild ____   Rest ____

Warm-up _____   **Cool-down** _____

Cross-training (specify) _____

Training Conditions

Location _____   **Time of day** _____

People   Trained alone ____   Trained w/partner ____   Trained w/group ____

Terrain _____   **Surface** _____

Temperature ____   **Humidity** ____   **Wind** ____   **Precipitation** _____

Training Grade for the Day

Physical status	A	B	C	D	F
Psychological status	A	B	C	D	F

Comments _____

_____

_____

Two New York City legends: nine-time winner Grete Waitz and race founder Fred Lebow finish together in 1992.

WEEK FIFTEEN:
Easing Back

Recovering from a marathon takes longer than one week—and possibly more than a month. Recovery passes through several stages, and you barely finish the first of those this week. That's the sore-muscle stage, which peaks on the *second* day afterward and disappears by week's end. The more subtle effects remain. Fatigue lingers, along with a sense of psychological letdown that runners call postmarathon blues. These take much longer to pass.

A popular rule of thumb says that the recovery period lasts one day per mile, or even a day per kilometer. That's a month to six weeks. What to do during that time? Run after the first few days, certainly. But keep the runs short and the pace easy; avoid all races. Don't schedule another marathon for yourself, or start training for one, until you satisfy all recovery requirements. Choose your program below, assign workouts to the next seven days' diary pages, and add details there for completed training.

Cruiser Program
Big day: none.
Other training days: three or four easy runs at whatever slow pace and short distance the legs allow.
Rest days: three to four with no running, but possibly cross-training.

Pacer Program
Big day: none.
Other training days: four to five easy runs at whatever slow pace and short distance the legs allow.
Rest days: two to three days with no running, but possibly cross-training.

Racer Program
Long day: none.
Fast day: none.
Other training days: four to six easy runs at whatever slow pace and short distance the legs allow.
Rest days: one to three with no running, but possibly cross-training.

Day 94

Thought for the Day

"PMS"

Those letters could stand for either *pre*marathon or *post*marathon syndrome. Beforehand you imagine you're sick or injured. Afterward you truly do suffer. I write today of the aftereffects.

Racing is an unnatural act, and this is especially true for marathons. They play some nasty tricks on the body, and the results last longer than we care to admit. The worst damage doesn't usually come from the marathon itself. The body seems to absorb that first punch pretty well. But the next one can be a killer. It lands when we rush back into full training too soon and we're still too weak to resist the second blow.

This is why one of the most important parts of the marathon-training program is also one of the most ignored. It's what to do for the next month or so *after* the race, which should be very little.

After one marathon, I came down with a virus. It was a particularly nasty strain that hit harder than anything I'd suffered in 25 years. It eliminated all running for more than a week, and didn't give up and go away completely for months.

I don't believe we catch viruses; they catch *us*. They always lurk about, waiting for our defenses to weaken. They're nature's way of telling us to slow down. I should have slowed down more, and longer, after the marathon. Just 11 days afterward, running seemed to be back to normal. That week, the illness struck. Germs weren't to blame; impatience was.

If we don't take enough recovery time voluntarily, the body will find its own way to get all it needs.

Tip for the Day

Be prepared for postrace pain. You can expect stiffness in the thighs and calves, and you can wear your limp as a badge of courage. Rest until this soreness disappears, which should take less than a week.

Day 94

Date _____

Plan _____

Training for the Day

Training Session

Type   Long ____   Fast ____   Easy ____   Other (specify) _____

Distance _____   **Time** _____

Pace _____   **Splits** _____ / _____ / _____ / _____ / _____

Effort   Max ____   Hard ____   Moderate ____   Mild ____   Rest ____

Warm-up _____   **Cool-down** _____

Cross-training (specify) _____

Training Conditions

Location _____   **Time of day** _____

People   Trained alone ____   Trained w/partner ____   Trained w/group ____

Terrain _____   **Surface** _____

Temperature ____   **Humidity** ____   **Wind** ____   **Precipitation** _____

Training Grade for the Day

Physical status   A   B   C   D   F

Psychological status   A   B   C   D   F

Comments _____

_____

_____

Day 95

Thought for the Day

How They Recover

You come off a hard race over the weekend. You let the immediate soreness and tiredness subside. Then you wonder, "Where do I go from here?"

Your race went one of two ways, and either can lead you to the same wrong conclusion. Either you did well and now think, "I could run even better if I trained more." Or you ran poorly and think, "I wouldn't have done so badly if I'd trained more."

Your conclusion isn't necessarily wrong, but the timing is if you start working harder immediately. Recovery isn't complete when acute muscle pain and fatigue ease, but has barely begun then.

Racing hurts, in ways both obvious and subtle. What you need right after a tough race isn't more training but less, and for more time than you might realize. Full recovery takes anywhere from several days to many weeks, depending on race distance. The longer you raced, the more time you must spend getting over it.

How much time? I asked the runners who presumably train the most and race the hardest. Eighty of them answered my questionnaire. A few of these runners barely acknowledge any need to recover. Top master Bob Schlau says, "I just keep going." American 10K record holder Mark Nenow would "back off intensity but not distance." Others insist on following a short race with a long run the next day. Tim Gargiulo, a 13:27 5K man, says, "I usually do as close to my normal Sunday run as possible, then perhaps cut back a few miles on Monday."

Most runners, however, take much longer to rebound. You're wise to err on the side of conservatism during the postmarathon period.

Tip for the Day

While resting, leave the marathon time on your watch and glance at it proudly. As you start to run again, notice the zeroing of time. The marathon is finished, and you're starting over in training.

Day 95

Date _____

Plan _____

Training for the Day

Training Session

Type   Long ____   Fast ____   Easy ____   Other (specify) _____

Distance _____   **Time** _____

Pace _____   **Splits** _____ / _____ / _____ / _____ / _____

Effort   Max ____   Hard ____   Moderate ____   Mild ____   Rest ____

Warm-up _____   **Cool-down** _____

Cross-training (specify) _____

Training Conditions

Location _____   **Time of day** _____

People   Trained alone ____   Trained w/partner ____   Trained w/group ____

Terrain _____   **Surface** _____

Temperature ____   **Humidity** ____   **Wind** ____   **Precipitation** _____

Training Grade for the Day

Physical status   A   B   C   D   F

Psychological status   A   B   C   D   F

Comments _____

_____

_____

Day 96

Thought for the Day

Softening the Focus

Jack Foster, who ran a 2:11 marathon at age 41, wrote 20 years ago of needing one easy day for each mile of the race. Today's athletes often allow a light week after a 10K and a month after a marathon.

Boston and New York City Marathon winner Miki Gorman took "slow, slow runs for a couple of days, then total rest for one or two days." Jacqueline Gareau and Greg Meyer, both Boston champions, say they simply reversed their prerace taper.

Besides juggling the amount and effort of running, these athletes try other therapies—both physical and mental. Cross-training, especially water work, is common during recovery. Many runners take massages. Some use ice or cold water to fight inflammation, while others try to soak out their soreness in hot tubs.

Several athletes mention diet changes. Dan Held, a 2:13 marathoner, says, "The key after a marathon is to refuel. Postrace carbo loading is as important as prerace." Runner-writer Don Kardong lists "hot fudge" as his favorite recovery food. Canadian Olympian Peter Maher likes his "Guinness and french fries."

After a big race, the runners break their routines. Gordon Bakoulis, a 2:33 marathoner, says, "I don't keep a log for two weeks." U.S. Olympian Julie Isphording will "make no plans, set no goals for a month." World marathon record holder Ingrid Kristiansen writes, "I use this time to do things I enjoy and normally don't have time to do."

The recovery period is when even the most focused runners take time to soften their focus.

Tip for the Day

Resist the urge to rush back into full training as soon as your leg soreness eases. You've only passed through the most obvious but shortest stage of recovery. Two subtle and longer-lasting stages remain.

Day 96

Date _____

Plan _____

Training for the Day

Training Session

Type   Long ____   Fast ____   Easy ____   Other (specify) _____

Distance _____   **Time** _____

Pace _____   **Splits** _____ / _____ / _____ / _____ / _____

Effort   Max ____   Hard ____   Moderate ____   Mild ____   Rest ____

Warm-up _____   **Cool-down** _____

Cross-training (specify) _____

Training Conditions

Location _____   **Time of day** _____

People   Trained alone ____   Trained w/partner ____   Trained w/group ____

Terrain _____   **Surface** _____

Temperature ____   **Humidity** ____   **Wind** ____   **Precipitation** _____

Training Grade for the Day

Physical status   A   B   C   D   F

Psychological status   A   B   C   D   F

Comments _____

_____

_____

Day 97

Thought for the Day

Stand and Deliver

This isn't news you want to hear anytime, let alone at 5:30 the morning after an otherwise satisfying day. "The kid didn't make it," said Pete League as I joined him at breakfast.

The "kid" was a 25-year-old marathoner capable of running well below three hours. He'd collapsed at the finish line of the Houston-Tenneco Marathon and had died of what doctors described as "a rare affliction that resulted in massive internal bleeding." Pete League had never met the young man and didn't see him fall. But the news hit Pete like a death in the family.

League founded this race in the early 1970s. He now serves as one of Director David Hannah's most trusted assistants, taking charge of the finish area in and around a convention center—including the medical team. League had gone three straight nights without much sleep, and his work wasn't finished yet. This Monday, he would collect statements from workers who'd witnessed the tragedy.

Pete handles his big job without asking for pay or fanfare. When we met on Saturday, he said, "I woke up at two o'clock this morning and couldn't get back to sleep. All these details were racing through my mind." We met that day at the finish line, where he'd been since dawn and would stay until after dark . . . then awaken again at two o'clock on raceday morning, be at his post by five, and not leave until late Sunday afternoon.

While staying with Pete and his wife, Lynn, that weekend, I hung out more than usual at ground zero. Watching the finish area come together and then come down was something every runner should do. It helps you appreciate what was done for you.

Tip for the Day

Observe the second stage of recovery: the more hungry, thirsty, sleepy feeling. When you run, it's like you're wearing 10-pound shoes. This stage takes several weeks to pass.

Day 97

Date _____

Plan _____

Training for the Day

Training Session

Type   Long ____   Fast ____   Easy ____   Other (specify) _____

Distance _____   **Time** _____

Pace _____   **Splits** _____ / _____ / _____ / _____ / _____

Effort   Max ____   Hard ____   Moderate ____   Mild ____   Rest ____

Warm-up _____   **Cool-down** _____

Cross-training (specify) _____

Training Conditions

Location _____   **Time of day** _____

People   Trained alone ____   Trained w/partner ____   Trained w/group ____

Terrain _____   **Surface** _____

Temperature ____   **Humidity** ____   **Wind** ____   **Precipitation** _____

Training Grade for the Day

Physical status   A   B   C   D   F

Psychological status   A   B   C   D   F

Comments _____

_____

_____

Day 98

Thought for the Day

Give Something Back

Peeking behind the scenes at the Houston-Tenneco Marathon reminded me of several truths:

- Running the race may be one of the easier jobs done that day. It takes less time than the set-up work that starts before the first runner arrives and ends long after the last one leaves.
- Runners as a group are quick to complain and slow to thank these workers. They gripe if T-shirts aren't the right size or the bananas aren't ripe, and expect someone else to clean up.
- Runners are transients, coming and going like replaceable parts. The Pete Leagues are the permanent fixtures who keep races running.

Runners would do well to practice a form of tithing. For every 10 races that they run, they should agree to work at one. Hand out race numbers, work an aid station, direct traffic, read mile splits, check in finishers, give away T-shirts, award the winners, or assist the injured. Doing this would help a sport that's always long on runners and short on helpers. It would also help the runner become quicker with the compliments.

Few runners in Houston noticed Pete League at work on raceday, let alone thanked him for his help. But he hadn't taken that job for applause. Pete helped for the best of reasons. He has been a runner for more than 40 years and has received this kind of assistance hundreds of times. Now graduated from his racing, he gives to others what he has so often received himself. He's one more of the many unsung heroes of this sport.

Tip for the Day

Observe the third stage of recovery: the psychological healing that often takes the longest. You can't think about running another marathon until you forget how hard the last one felt.

Day 98

Date _____

Plan _____

Training for the Day

Training Session

Type   Long ____   Fast ____   Easy ____   Other (specify) _____

Distance _____   **Time** _____

Pace _____   **Splits** _____ / _____ / _____ / _____ / _____

Effort   Max ____   Hard ____   Moderate ____   Mild ____   Rest ____

Warm-up _____   **Cool-down** _____

Cross-training (specify) _____

Training Conditions

Location _____   **Time of day** _____

People   Trained alone ____   Trained w/partner ____   Trained w/group ____

Terrain _____   **Surface** _____

Temperature ____   **Humidity** ____   **Wind** ____   **Precipitation** _____

Training Grade for the Day

Physical status   A   B   C   D   F

Psychological status   A   B   C   D   F

Comments _____

_____

_____

Day 99

Thought for the Day

Names and Faces

If you only want the facts about a race, save yourself a trip. Stay home and order a list of names and places to read. But if you want to put faces with those names and voices with the faces, you have to be there in person. That's the only way to take the people personally.

Flory Rodd, then an airline navigator in his early 40s, ran his first race at the 1967 Boston Marathon. It wasn't just his first at that distance but his first at *any* distance.

Rodd went to Boston not knowing anyone in the Boston field. By nature a collector of friends, he made many new ones that weekend. I too made Boston my first marathon that year. I went there knowing few of the runners, and most of those only by name.

Rodd took home copies of the entry and results lists published in the *Globe*. I didn't save those papers. One summer a quarter century later, I visited Flory and his wife, Gail. They showed me an old scrapbook. Through the years, Flory had highlighted with a colored pen the names of runners who'd since become his friends.

Flory lent me those colorful pages for copying. I'm now looking at a list marked as his was—with names that have taken on faces, voices, and personalities. The number right after mine belonged to a Dr. G. A. Sheehan from New Jersey. The next year, he became "George" when we met at the Mexico City Olympics. Soon after that, he became one of the best friends I—or this sport—have ever known.

Tip for the Day

Once the initial euphoria of finishing wears off, expect to encounter the postmarathon blues. This is a weariness of spirit, and the idea of running any distance at any pace doesn't excite you.

Day 99

Date _____

Plan _____

Training for the Day

Training Session

Type   Long ____   Fast ____   Easy ____   Other (specify) _____

Distance _____   **Time** _____

Pace _____   **Splits** _____ / _____ / _____ / _____ / _____

Effort   Max ____   Hard ____   Moderate ____   Mild ____   Rest ____

Warm-up _____   **Cool-down** _____

Cross-training (specify) _____

Training Conditions

Location _____   **Time of day** _____

People   Trained alone ____   Trained w/partner ____   Trained w/group ____

Terrain _____   **Surface** _____

Temperature ____   **Humidity** ____   **Wind** ____   **Precipitation** _____

Training Grade for the Day

Physical status   A   B   C   D   F

Psychological status   A   B   C   D   F

Comments _____

_____

_____

Day 100

Thought for the Day

Name Game

What strikes me most from the old list of finishers from my first marathon, Boston 1967, is how many of these friends became writers and how much we've all written since 1967. Amby Burfoot and Ed Ayres would later edit two national monthly magazines. Tom Osler had just written a training booklet then that would become a classic. Hal Higdon, Ron Daws, Dave Prokop, and Peter Wood all would publish running books in the 1970s.

In the 1980s, Gabe Mirkin would become a sports-medicine author, Frank Zarnowski a decathlon resource, and Peter Mundle a keeper of age-group records. In the 1990s, Tom Derderian would write the definitive history of the Boston Marathon. The best-known name from that Boston, Kathrine Switzer, has a book in progress. Erich Segal wouldn't write running books but best-selling novels, starting with *Love Story*.

Recently Flory Rodd, who'd run that 1967 Boston, highlighted a new name-turned-friend in his scrapbook. The meeting came while Rodd visited New Zealand. Flory dropped in unannounced to see Dave McKenzie, who'd won that race. "I was afraid of getting him into trouble, taking up all his time at work," says Flory. "But as our running talk got thicker, he began pulling old running pictures and Boston mementos out of his office desk."

The memories had grown in value with age. The distance between the first man on the old Boston results sheet and the 184th had shrunk when these two runners added faces and voices to the names.

Tip for the Day

Treat "PMS"—or postmarathon syndrome—as a useful natural phenomenon that is both physical and psychological. You're still recovering, and your body and psyche aren't yet ready for a new goal as compelling as the last.

Day 100

Date _____

Plan _____

Training for the Day

Training Session

Type   Long ____   Fast ____   Easy ____   Other (specify) _____

Distance _____   **Time** _____

Pace _____   **Splits** _____ / _____ / _____ / _____ / _____

Effort   Max ____   Hard ____   Moderate ____   Mild ____   Rest ____

Warm-up _____   **Cool-down** _____

Cross-training (specify) _____

Training Conditions

Location _____   **Time of day** _____

People   Trained alone ____   Trained w/partner ____   Trained w/group ____

Terrain _____   **Surface** _____

Temperature ____   **Humidity** ____   **Wind** ____   **Precipitation** _____

Training Grade for the Day

Physical status   A   B   C   D   F

Psychological status   A   B   C   D   F

Comments _____

_____

_____

Cheers! Drink stations are a welcome sight and a physical necessity at all marathons, especially in balmy Honolulu.

100 MARATHONS

Where to run your next marathon? Your choices number in the hundreds, and this without even leaving the North American continent. *Runner's World* magazine lists more than 250 races each year in the United States and Canada, plus dozens more around the world. They appear on nearly every weekend of any year.

Following are 100 of the best marathons, with at least one from each state and province, along with all races with 25 or more years of history. Information includes name of the marathon, location, usual month of its running, and an address to write for details. Check each January *Runner's World* for updates.

UNITED STATES

ALABAMA—Rocket City Marathon, Huntsville (December): 8811 Edgehill Dr., Huntsville, AL 35802.

ALASKA—Equinox Marathon, Fairbanks (September): Box 84237, Fairbanks, AK 99708 . . . Mayor's Midnight Sun, Anchorage (June): Box 196650, Anchorage, AK 99519.

ARIZONA—Valley of the Sun Marathon, Phoenix (February): 6505 N. 16th St., Phoenix, AZ 85069.

ARKANSAS—Arkansas Marathon, Booneville (November): Second & Bennett, Booneville, AR 72927.

CALIFORNIA—Avenue of the Giants Marathon, Weott (May): 281 Hidden Valley Rd., Bayside, CA 95524 . . . Big Sur International Marathon, Carmel (April): Box 222620, Carmel, CA 93922 . . . California International Marathon, Sacramento (December): Box 161149, Sacramento, CA 95816 . . . Los Angeles Marathon (March): 11101 W. Ohio Ave., Ste. 100, Los Angeles, CA 90025 . . . Napa Valley Marathon, Napa (March): Box 4307, Napa, CA 94558 . . . Palos Verdes Marathon (June): Box 2856, Palos Verdes, CA 90274 . . . San Diego Marathon (January): 511-A Cedros Ave., Ste. B, Solana Beach, CA 92075 . . . San Francisco

Marathon (July): Box 77148, San Francisco, CA 94107 . . . Western Hemisphere Marathon, Culver City (December): 4117 Overland Ave., Culver City, CA 90230.

COLORADO—Colorado Marathon, Denver (October): 2126 S. Kalamath, Denver, CO 80233 . . . Pike's Peak Marathon, Manitou Springs (August): Box 38235, Colorado Springs, CO 80937.

CONNECTICUT—Hartford Marathon (October): 221 Main St., Hartford, CT 06106.

DELAWARE—Delaware Marathon, Middletown (December): Box 398, Wilmington, DE 19899.

DISTRICT OF COLUMBIA—Marine Corps Marathon, Washington (October): Box 188, Quantico, VA 22134.

FLORIDA—Walt Disney World Marathon, Orlando (January): Box 10,000, Lake Buena Vista, FL 32830.

GEORGIA—Atlanta Marathon (November): 3097 E. Shadowlawn Ave., Atlanta, GA 30305.

HAWAII—Honolulu Marathon (December): 3435 Wailae Ave., Ste. 208, Honolulu, HI 96816 . . . Maui Marathon, Kahului (March): Box 330099, Kahului, HI 96733.

IDAHO—Coeur d'Alene Marathon (May): Box 2393, Coeur d'Alene, ID 83816.

ILLINOIS—Chicago Marathon (October): 54 W. Hubbard St., Chicago, IL 60610 . . . Lake County Marathon, Zion (April): Box 9, Highland Park, IL 60035.

INDIANA—Sunburst Marathon, South Bend (June): 615 N. Michigan St., South Bend, IN 46601.

IOWA—University of Okoboji Marathon, Pike's Point State Park (July): Box 3077, Spencer, IA 51301.

KANSAS—Wichita Marathon (October): 393 N. McLean Blvd., Wichita, KS 67203.

KENTUCKY—Kentucky Marathon, Louisville (December): 7004 Beachlands Beach, Prospect, KY 40059.

LOUISIANA—Mardi Gras Marathon, New Orleans (January): Box 52003, New Orleans, LA 70152.

MAINE—Maine Marathon, Portland (October): Box 8654, Portland, ME 04104.

MARYLAND—Washington's Birthday Marathon, Greenbelt (February): Box 1352, Arlington, VA 22210.

MASSACHUSETTS—Boston Athletic Association Marathon (April): Box 1996, Hopkinton, MA 01748 . . . Race of Champions Marathon, Holyoke (May): 231 Elm St., West Springfield, MA 01089.

MICHIGAN—Detroit Free Press Marathon, Detroit (October): 300 Stroh River Pl., Ste. 4000, Detroit, MI 48207.

MINNESOTA—Grandma's Marathon, Duluth (June): Box 16234, Duluth, MN 55816 . . . Twin Cities Marathon, Minneapolis-St. Paul (October): 708 N. First St., Ste. CR-33, Minneapolis, MN 55401.

MISSISSIPPI—Tupelo Marathon (September): 1007 Chester Ave., Tupelo, MS 38801.

MISSOURI—Heart of America Marathon, Columbia (September): Box 1872, Columbia, MO 65205 . . . Olympiad Memorial Marathon, St. Louis (February): 13453 Chesterfield Plaza, Chesterfield, MO 63017.

MONTANA—Governor's Cup Marathon, Helena (May): Box 451, Helena, MT 59624.

NEBRASKA—Lincoln Marathon (May): 5309 S. 62nd St., Lincoln, NE 68516 . . . Omaha Riverfront Marathon, Omaha (November): 5822 Ohio St., Omaha, NE 68104.

NEVADA—Las Vegas International Marathon, Las Vegas (February): Box 81262, Las Vegas, NV 89180.

NEW HAMPSHIRE—Clarence DeMar Marathon, Gilsam (September): Box 6257, Keene, NH 03431.

NEW JERSEY—Atlantic City Marathon (October): Box 2181, Ventnor, NJ 08406.

NEW MEXICO—Duke City Marathon, Albuquerque (September): Box 4543, Albuquerque, NM 87196.

NEW YORK—Buffalo Marathon (May): Box 652, Buffalo, NY 14202 . . . Long Island Marathon, East Meadow (May): Sports

Unit, Eisenhower Park, East Meadow, NY 11554 . . . New York City Marathon (November): 9 E. 89th St., New York, NY 10128 . . . Yonkers Marathon (October): 285 Nepperhan Ave., Yonkers, NY 10701.

NORTH CAROLINA—Charlotte Observer Marathon, Charlotte (February): Box 30294, Charlotte, NC 28230 . . . Grandfather Mountain Marathon, Boone (July): 460 Deerfield Forest Pkwy., Boone, NC 28607.

NORTH DAKOTA—Bismarck Marathon (September): Box 549, Bismarck, ND 58502.

OHIO—Athens Marathon (March): 44 Grosvenor St., Athens, OH 45701 . . . Columbus Marathon (November): Box 26806, Columbus, OH 43226 . . . Glass City Marathon, Toledo (April): 130 Yale Dr., Toledo, OH 43614 . . . Revco Cleveland Marathon (May): 1925 Enterprise Pkwy., Twinsburg, OH 44087.

OKLAHOMA—Gage Roadrunner Marathon, Gage (May): Box 328, Gage, OK 73843 . . . Tulsa (November): 263 E. 45th Pl., Tulsa, OK 74105.

OREGON—Portland Marathon (September): Box 4040, Beaverton, OR 97076 . . . Trail's End Marathon, Seaside (March): Box 549, Beaverton, OR 97075.

PENNSYLVANIA—City of Pittsburgh Marathon (May): 4601 Baum Blvd., Pittsburgh, PA 15213 . . . Philadelphia Marathon (November): Box 21601, Philadelphia, PA 19131.

RHODE ISLAND—Ocean State Marathon, Narragansett (November): 5 Division St., East Greenwich, RI 02818.

SOUTH CAROLINA—Carolina Marathon, Columbia (February): Box 5092, Columbia, SC 29250.

SOUTH DAKOTA—Longest Day Marathon, Brookings (April): 410 Fourth St., Brookings, SD 57006.

TENNESSEE—Memphis Marathon (December): Box 84, Memphis, TN 38101.

TEXAS—Austin Marathon (February): Box 684456, Austin, TX 78768 . . . Cowtown Marathon, Fort Worth (February): Box 9066, Fort Worth, TX 76147 . . . Dallas White Rock Marathon, Dallas (December): 3607 Oak Lawn, Dallas, TX 75219 . . . Houston-

Tenneco Marathon, Houston (January): 5900 Memorial Dr., Ste. 200, Houston, TX 77007.

UTAH—Deseret News Marathon, Salt Lake City (July): Box 1257, Salt Lake City, UT 84110 . . . St. George Marathon (October): 86 S. Main St., St. George, UT 84770.

VERMONT—Green Mountain Marathon, South Hero (October): 6010 Main Rd., Huntington, VT 02462.

VIRGINIA—Shamrock Marathon, Virginia Beach (March): 2308 Maple St., Virginia Beach, VA 23451.

WASHINGTON—Capital City Marathon, Olympia (May): Box 1681, Olympia, WA 98507 . . . Seattle Marathon (November): Box 31849, Seattle, WA 98103.

WEST VIRGINIA—Almost Heaven Marathon, Charleston (December): 19 Riverside Dr., South Charleston, WV 25303.

WISCONSIN—Fox Cities Marathon, Neenah (October): 835 Valley Rd., Menasha, WI 54952 . . . Lakefront Marathon, Milwaukee (October): 9200 W. North Ave., Milwaukee, WI 53226 . . . Paavo Nurmi Marathon, Upson (August): 207 Silver St., Hurley, WI 54534.

WYOMING—Wyoming Marathon, Laramie (May): 3204 Reed Ave., Cheyenne, WY 82001.

CANADA

ALBERTA—Calgary Stampede Marathon, Calgary (July): Box 296, Station M, Calgary, AL T2P 2H9, Canada . . . Edmonton Festival Marathon, Edmonton (August): 8537 109th St., Edmonton, AL T6G 1E4, Canada.

BRITISH COLUMBIA—Okanagan International Marathon, Kelowna (May): 115-2463 Hwy. 99N, Kelowna, BC V1X 4S2, Canada . . . Royal Victoria Marathon, Victoria (October): 182-911 Yates St., Victoria, BC V8V 4X3, Canada . . . Vancouver International Marathon, Vancouver (May): Box 3213, Vancouver, BC V6B 3X8, Canada.

MANITOBA—Manitoba Marathon, Winnipeg (June): 200 Main St., Winnipeg, MN R3C 4M2, Canada.

NEW BRUNSWICK—Festival by the Sea Marathon, St. John (August): 50 Union St., St. John, NB E2L 1A1, Canada.

NEWFOUNDLAND—Twin Cities Marathon, St. Johns (September): 47 Victory Ln., Mount Pearl, NF A1N 3Z3, Canada.

NORTHWEST TERRITORIES—Midnight Sun Marathon, Baffin Island (June): 20 Toronto St., 12th F., Toronto, ON M5C 2B8, Canada.

NOVA SCOTIA—Johnny Miles Marathon, New Glasgow (May): Box 7, New Glasgow, NS B2H 5E1, Canada.

ONTARIO—Canadian International Marathon, Toronto (October): RR 1, Uxbridge, ON L9P 1R1, Canada . . . National Capital Marathon (May): Box 426, Station A, Ottawa, ON K1N 8V5, Canada

PRINCE EDWARD ISLAND—Prince Edward Island Marathon, Charlottetown (September): 252 Prince St., Charlottetown, PEI C1A 4S1, Canada.

QUEBEC—Montreal Marathon (September): Box 1383, Station Place d'Ames, Montreal, PQ H2Y 3K5, Canada.

SASKATCHEWAN—Saskatchewan Marathon, Saskatoon (September): 128 Ottawa St. S., Saskatoon, SA S7M 3L5, Canada.

YUKON—Yukon Gold Midnight Marathon, Whitehorse (June): 4061 Fourth Ave., Whitehorse, YK Y1A 1H1, Canada.

ABOUT THE AUTHOR

Joe Henderson has been writing about running for more than 30 years. He's not only the West Coast editor and a featured columnist for *Runner's World* magazine but also the author of more than a dozen books on running, including *Better Runs*, *Long-Run Solution*, *Fitness Running*, and *Jog, Run, Race*. A veteran runner who has completed more than 40 marathons in his life, Henderson has seen firsthand how the event's popularity has grown and has played an important role in developing marathon training techniques. He popularized the training method known as "LSD" (long, slow distance) as well as the now common practice of taking walking breaks during marathons.

After receiving his BA from Drake University in 1965, Henderson worked as an editor in the sports department at the *Des Moines Register* and later as a staff writer for *Track & Field News*. In 1967 he started his long employment with *Runner's World*, where he eventually worked his way up to senior editor. In addition, he writes and produces a monthly newsletter called *Running Commentary* and is an adjunct assistant professor of journalism at the University of Oregon.

Henderson is a former executive director of the International Runners Committee, which was instrumental in placing a women's marathon in the Olympics. His honors include being inducted into the Road Runners Club of America Hall of Fame and receiving the club's journalism award in 1979. He was named a Drake University Distinguished Alumnus in 1981. Henderson lives in Eugene, Oregon.

THE JOE HENDERSON LIBRARY

MARATHON TRAINING
The Proven 100-Day Program for Success
Includes Daily Training
JOE HENDERS

BETTER RUNS
25 YEARS' WORTH OF LESSONS FOR RUNNING FASTER AND FARTHER
FOREWORD BY JEFF GALLOWAY
HENDERSON

Fitness RUNNING
Richard L. Brown
Joe Henderson
FITNESS SPECTRUM SERIES